THE DATENIGHT
COOKBOOK

MEREDITH PHILLIPS

THE
DATENIGHT
COOKBOOK
romantic recipes for
the busy couple

TERRACE PUBLISHING

The Date Night Cookbook: romantic recipes for the busy couple

Copyright © 2008 The Meredith Phillips Company

All rights reserved. No part of this book may be reproduced in any form or by any electronic or mechanical means without written permission from the publisher.

To learn more about Meredith Phillips and *The Date Night Cookbook*, visit www.MeredithPhillips.com | www.TheDateNightCookbook.com

International Standard Book Number

ISBN-10: 095327574 | ISBN-13: 9780965327572

Library of Congress Control Number 2007906988

Written by Meredith Phillips

Packaged and Co-Published in the United States by Terrace Publishing | www.terracepartners.com

Distributed by Terrace Publishing through IPG

Project Development: **Denise Vivaldo**

Managing Editor: **Martha Hopkins**

Editorial Assistance: **Gwyneth Doland, Kristen Green Wiewora, and Lisa Asher**

Book Design: **Randall Lockridge**

Photography: **Jon Edwards and Associates**

Food Styling: **Denise Vivaldo and Cindie Flannigan of Food Fanatics**

Photography Art Direction: **Matt Armendariz**

Photography Assistance: **Adam Pearson**

Distributed to the book trade in the United States and Canada by:

Independent Publishers Group

814 North Franklin Street

Chicago, IL 60610

312.337.0747

www.ipgbook.com

Printed in China | Foreign Rights Available | First Edition

10 9 8 7 6 5 4 3 2 1

for fritz

acknowledgments

In creating this cookbook, I have learned that writing is but one component of the publishing process. Behind every author is a team of dedicated, passionate people required to bring a finished book to fruition. I want to thank those who have worked tirelessly to make my cookbook dream a reality.

So, an enthusiastic thank-you to Denise Vivaldo of Food Fanatics, for your picture-perfect food styling and gracious support and guidance from day one. To Cindie Flannigan, for your detailed recipe testing and encyclopedic knowledge of food. To Jon Edwards, for making my recipes come to mouth-watering life through your lens. To Matt Armendariz and Adam Pearson, for your assistance on the shoot and impeccable eye for all things beautiful. To Gwyneth Doland and Kristen Green Wiewora, for making my words sing. To Randall Lockridge, for your clean, approachable design. To Martha Hopkins of Terrace Publishing, thank you for taking on this massive project with enthusiasm and vigor. You have truly steered the *Date Night* ship through the complicated waters of publishing. I am glad to be along for the ride.

Thanks as well to Mom and Dad, for letting me tag along on your culinary adventures and never hindering mine. To Matty, for putting up a fair fight over licking the spoon (well, sort of). To Nana, for showing me the beauty in a simple game of cards, a slice of strudel, and a good, strong cup of Folgers. To Bob and Betsy, for providing the beautiful backdrop and welcoming me into the family. To Fritz, who always makes our food look better, smell better, taste better. Thank you for inspiring *Date Night* and *our* date night. I love you.

— M.P. 2007

table of contents

foreword

If there's anything we love more than food and wine, it's enjoying them with each other.

When the galleys for this book arrived on our doorstep on our 17th wedding anniversary, we believed it fate that we accept the accompanying invitation to write its Foreword. And as a couple who has long managed to weather the challenges of both working and living together, we're only too happy to advocate cooking a *deux* as one of the two most enjoyable ways we know for couples to experience sensuous pleasures together.

Our mutual enjoyment of food has been central to our relationship since our very first dinner together the night we met in 1985, sitting side by side at an Italian restaurant eating pasta with red sauce and Chianti. We subsequently dated long-distance for two years. To us, food was not just the backdrop of our courtship; it emerged as a key expression of our growing affection. Andrew knew Karen—who cooks only rarely—was the one for him after she lovingly made him *spaghetti alla carbonara* for dinner and French-pressed coffee for breakfast in New York. And Karen fell for Andrew because if he knew he'd still be working late at the restaurant by the time her train pulled into Boston's South Station, he'd leave her dinner in the refrigerator at his apartment with a love note taped to a split of wine.

Our work has introduced us to numerous extraordinary dining experiences, many at some of America's most romantic restaurants—from Daniel in New York City to the Inn at Little Washington in Virginia.

But it's the meals we've enjoyed in our own Manhattan apartment that have brought the most *joie de vivre* into our lives on a day-to-day basis. From the sizzle of salmon hitting the sauté pan and the pop of the Pinot Noir being uncorked, the sounds and smells and tastes shared while cooking at home together can create a feeling of closeness and intimacy like nothing else. Even on a night you don't feel like cooking, selecting the right combination of food and wine can create magic: One of our favorite Valentine's Day dinners of all time was staying in bed all night sipping chilled Neige ice cider (a Canadian wine made from apples) with an array of cheeses, pâtés, and breads while watching a double-feature of romantic comedies. Heaven!

Food can also help to soothe the "lovers' quarrels" that inevitably arise in any relationship—especially between two strong personalities such as our own. After one stupid fight we had over who-knows-what, Andrew stormed off to the bathroom to take a shower while both our tempers cooled. Karen found it easier to make peace through food than through words: When Andrew stepped out of the bathroom, he couldn't help but smile to find a big heart on the floor in front of him formed out of a dozen Hershey's chocolate kisses.

Like you, no doubt, we have a long list of our favorite make-at-home meals. But even professional chefs (as Andrew is) and culinary authors (as we both have been these past dozen years) get into ruts. When it's time to spark some new ideas, it is always helpful to take a look through other books and to find out what other couples are making and eating at home. With Meredith Phillips' *Date Night Cookbook*, it's actually possible to do both. We're happy to glean tips that might transport us to France for the night (page 117's Bouillabaisse, which we'd accompany with a favorite Provençal rosé), or simply allow us to enjoy a more casual "date night" supper (page 83's Halibut Tacos with Chipotle Sour Cream with its recommended "ice-cold bucket of beer").

Meredith's Roasted Cauliflower Soup (page 65) caught Andrew's eye, which tickled cauliflower-loving Karen, as it took her years of coaxing to get Andrew to even try it (but he clearly liked it!). As it happens, Meredith had the *exact* same problem with Fritz, but he's now a convert, too. The Coconut-Almond Candy Bars (page 125) made Karen's mouth water, but as Andrew is not keen on coconut, it may never come to pass in our home. After all, we'd rather eat any dish together than enjoy a favorite dish apart.

Here's wishing you and your own date happy cooking—and happy eating!

—*Andrew Dornenburg and Karen Page*
husband + wife, and award-winning co-authors of *Becoming a Chef, Culinary Artistry, Dining Out, Chef's Night Out, The New American Chef,* and *What to Drink with What You Eat*

Andrew and Karen's Secrets to Date Night Cooking

+ Cook with love!

+ Know each other's strengths and use them to your mutual advantage. As a former restaurant chef, Andrew cooks everything fast and on high heat. As a recovering perfectionist, Karen inspects every single ingredient—from salad greens to berries—to make sure they're perfect, and will only use the very best. So, when we make waffles, Karen measures the dry ingredients precisely, while Andrew whips the egg whites in record time.

+ Let the other person complete their assigned task—and only then offer advice and opinion, if necessary. Or, better yet, offer feedback only if requested.

+ Respect each other's preferences. Karen's version of al dente pasta or vegetables is a bit softer than Andrew's version, so we compromise by cooking them exactly in the middle.

+ Don't forget to set a romantic table, complete with candles and/or flowers, a complementary wine, and music.

+ P.S. from Andrew, the professional chef: If your date adds salt at the table to the dish you just slaved in the kitchen to create, it does NOT mean that she doesn't love you.

introduction

This is a book for couples who love life, love food, and love spending time together—with what little free time they have. People today seem so much busier than they were in our parents' and grandparents' generations. It's hard to make time to cook a meal at home, and almost irresistibly easy just to let someone else do it for us. Every day there's a new survey showing an ever-increasing percentage of meals Americans are eating in their cars and an ever-decreasing percentage of meals we're eating at home. I hope this book will help you start to reverse that trend in your own lives.

Believe me, I understand how hard it can be for two people with hectic lives to somehow find time to be home together for dinner—and that's without adding children to the mix. When I was in the fashion industry, I subsisted almost exclusively on the catering trays provided on the sets for our 14-hour shoots. When I was on ABC's *The Bachelor* and *The Bachelorette* television shows, I craved the comfort of matzo ball soup from Jerry's Deli in LA. Somehow, those bowls of soup provided me a little oasis of calm during those hectic months. I ordered it take-out almost every single day.

But since then, everything has changed. Three years ago I decided to go to culinary school. I had always loved food, but I gradually realized that there wasn't anything else that I wanted to do with my life and my career. I wanted to cook, eat, and learn everything there is to know about food. I didn't learn *everything*, but I learned a lot. And I met someone special.

It was a Tuesday night, pouring rain, for our first night of class. I was late and wet from the downpour, and altogether making quite a spectacle of myself as the last student to arrive on that all-important first day of school. The teacher paired Fritz and me as cooking partners, and we plunged into our assignment: preparing the five mother sauces of Escoffier. We whisked and skimmed and reduced our way through a béchamel, velouté, espagnole, tomato, and a hollandaise.

And by the end of the class, I knew I was in trouble.

I had not gone to cooking school expecting love, but here it was. We started meeting before class at Beacon, a little Asian restaurant across from school, to share an appetizer and enjoy a glass of wine. As the weeks passed, we moved our meeting time earlier and earlier, sharing food and friendship until the very last second before class started.

After culinary school, Fritz and I both wanted to make cooking dinner at home a priority, so two years ago, we decided to schedule a date night: one night out of the week when we wouldn't make any other plans, when we would commit to no meetings, no classes, no errands, nothing but each other. And on this one night we wouldn't go out for dinner and a movie; we would stay home and cook for ourselves. We chose Tuesday, the same night we met. I think it is some of the most valuable time we spend together.

When we're cooking, we have fun, which is so important in a relationship. In the kitchen I'm reminded how well we balance each other. Before I met him, it would have really bothered me if something went wrong with a dish while I was cooking. I'm always looking for perfection in a dish, where Fritz is the encourager. Now, when something goes wrong, he always says the right thing: "Forget it! Let's have a glass of wine and order pizza!" He helps me remember it's not all about the food; it's about us.

Food is about nourishing people, but cooking together is about nourishing your relationship.

The food we cook on date night is all about ingredients, flavor, and fun, not about fancy names or elaborate presentation. I have filled these pages with the basics, the foods I love to cook every night like the Roasted Chicken with New Potatoes (my favorite), the Heirloom Tomato Salad with Feta and Balsamic Vinegar (his favorite), and the Asian Ground Turkey Lettuce Cups (our favorite). We cook in a way that fits us, and you should do the same. I never use a recipe to cook, while Fritz follows them to the letter. I like to put on a big pot of soup; Fritz likes to chop. I'm drawn to the lettuces and fresh herbs from our garden, while Fritz could live indefinitely on bread and cheese and steak, with a nice Cab on the side. Our tastes and styles happily intermingle, especially on date night, because it's done together and with love.

In this book you won't find many things too hard or too impractical to prepare on a busy Monday night. For the more time-consuming dishes, most all can be made the night or weekend before, reheated easily when you get home from work. And remember, when you're cooking together, the prep work takes half the time it would if you were cooking alone. So while he's making the dressing for the Caesar Salad, you can be tearing the lettuce. And while he's searing the steak, you can be mashing the Blue Cheese Mashed Potatoes. The more you cook together, the faster you'll get. And the more date nights you share, the more you'll nourish your growing relationship. Enjoy.

chapter one appetizers

Have you ever rolled your own spring rolls, made gyoza from scratch, or carefully seared ahi tuna? Appetizers, like first dates, allow you to explore, investigate, maybe try something new (and a little crazy?) without any fear of commitment. If you had the opportunity to go to dinner with a movie star or an astronaut, you'd do it just to check it out, wouldn't you? The same sense of fearless curiosity is what leads people to order things like escargot for the first time. Chefs know this, and they'll often put their most creative dishes, in miniature form, on the appetizer menu. The adventure in my appetizers lies partly in eating them, but mostly in making them together.

bruschetta three ways

In our backyard, we have a little vegetable garden. In the summer, our tomatoes and basil make a knockout pair. Roasted red peppers and feta are strong and tangy in the fall. In the winter, when it's impossible to find a decent tomato, we revel in the contrasting flavors of tangy goat cheese and sweet honey.

ingredients

prep time: 20 minutes | *cooking time:* 15 minutes | *yields:* 4 servings

basil and tomato bruschetta

2   small ripe tomatoes, seeded and diced

1   small bunch fresh basil, chopped

3   tablespoons extra-virgin olive oil

1   teaspoon minced fresh garlic

Kosher salt and freshly ground black pepper to taste

8   Crostini (page 25)

roasted red pepper and feta bruschetta

1   red bell pepper

3   tablespoons crumbled feta cheese

Kosher salt and freshly ground black pepper to taste

8   Crostini (page 25)

goat cheese and honey bruschetta

4   tablespoons goat cheese

2   tablespoons honey

8   Crostini (page 25)

variations

Dice fresh mozzarella with the tomatoes. Add grilled zucchini to the red pepper. Sprinkle toasted walnuts on the goat cheese and honey.

basil and tomato bruschetta

Combine the tomatoes, basil, olive oil, garlic, salt, and pepper in a small bowl. Let stand for 5 minutes. Spoon the mixture evenly among the Crostini.

roasted red pepper and feta bruschetta

Preheat the oven to 450 degrees. Place the bell pepper directly on a rack in the oven with a sheet pan placed on the rack below to catch any juices. Roast for 15 minutes, or until the skin darkens and begins to char. Alternatively, set the pepper directly above the flame on a gas stovetop. Turn with metal tongs until each side is blackened.

Place the charred pepper in a plastic or paper bag, seal, and let steam for 5 minutes. When the pepper is cool enough to handle, rub away the blackened skin with your hands—it's okay if a few bits remain. Discard the seeds, core, and membrane from the pepper, and slice the roasted flesh into thin strips.

Top the Crostini with the strips of red pepper and sprinkle evenly with the feta. Season with salt and pepper.

goat cheese and honey bruschetta

Spread each Crostini with ½ tablespoon of goat cheese and drizzle with honey.

buffalo chicken satay

This recipe combines the best of Buffalo wings with the satisfying serving method of skewered Thai satay. Nibbling on satay looks so much more refined than chowing on chicken wings, but the spicy-tangy dressing still delivers that Buffalo-wing kick everyone loves. Serve these with plenty of carrot and celery sticks.

prep time: 10 minutes | *cooking & marinating:* 35 minutes | *yields:* 4 servings

Slice the chicken breasts lengthwise into ¼-inch strips. Place the butter and hot sauce in a medium bowl and whisk to combine. Add the chicken strips and toss to coat. Cover and refrigerate for 30 minutes to marinate.

Prepare a hot grill, or preheat the broiler on high. Thread the chicken strips on metal or wooden skewers. (If using wood, be sure to soak in water for 30 minutes prior to using to keep them from burning.) Grill or broil about 3 minutes. Turn once and cook another 2 or 3 minutes, or until done. Serve with the Buttermilk Blue Cheese Dressing (page 55).

ingredients

- 1 pound boneless, skinless chicken breasts
- 8 tablespoons (1 stick) unsalted butter, melted
- ⅓ cup Frank's Red Hot Sauce, or your favorite hot sauce
- Buttermilk Blue Cheese Dressing for dipping (page 55)

variations

Try ranch dressing instead of blue cheese, or lemon zest, Parmesan, and black pepper instead of the hot sauce.

classic guacamole

Nothing that comes from a can, jar, or packet can imitate the silky richness, buttery flavor, or bright-green color of guacamole homemade with ripe avocados. If needed, allow the avocados to ripen for a day or two inside a paper bag on the counter. Cut avocados discolor quickly, so make this right before serving, and press plastic wrap down on top of it to prevent oxidation.

ingredients

prep time: 10 minutes | *yields:* 4 servings

2 ripe avocados

3 tablespoons freshly squeezed lime juice (about 2 to 3 medium limes)

1 medium tomato, seeded and diced

¼ red onion, finely diced

½ jalapeño, seeded and minced

½ teaspoon kosher salt

Dash of Tabasco or your favorite hot sauce

Slice the avocados in half, remove the pit, and scoop out the flesh. Mash the flesh coarsely with a fork and sprinkle with the lime juice. Add the tomato, onion, jalapeño, salt, and Tabasco. Stir with the fork until just combined. Taste and add more salt if needed.

variations

Chopped cilantro and green onions go nicely. Replace the lime juice with lemon. Vary the heat by adding more or less jalapeño and Tabasco.

sesame-crusted ahi

This Japanese-inspired starter requires high-quality ahi (yellowfin) tuna, suitable to eat rare, which you can find at fish markets and Asian markets. You can substitute frozen ahi, but it will lose some of its moisture and fine texture when defrosted. For an appetizer, we serve the seared fish with a lightly dressed cucumber salad—try the one on page 40—but a pot of sticky rice can easily make a meal of it.

prep time: 5 minutes | *cooking time:* 2 minutes | *yields:* 2 servings

Pour the sesame seeds on a plate and coat the tuna with the seeds on all sides, pressing to help them adhere.

Set a medium sauté pan over medium-high heat and add the oil. When the oil is hot, carefully lay the fish in the pan. Cook for 30 seconds without moving, and then turn and cook an additional 30 seconds on the other side. Remove from the pan and slice the tuna in ¼-inch-thick slices diagonally. The tuna will be raw and barely warm in the middle.

Serve with the soy sauce and wasabi for dipping, along with white sticky rice for a light lunch or dinner for two.

ingredients

3 tablespoons black or white sesame seeds

½ pound Ahi tuna

2 tablespoons canola oil

Soy sauce for dipping

Wasabi paste for dipping

variations

This same recipe can be made with black or white sesame seeds, a combination of both, or none at all.

salsa cruda

This uncooked salsa bursts with summer flavor. The recipe is infinitely flexible, so feel free to improvise with whatever's in season: yellow pear tomatoes, Vidalia onions, habanero chiles, or fresh oregano would all work well. This salsa is excellent when scooped up with warmed tortilla chips and washed down with an icy-cold margarita. If you have any left over, serve it the following morning on poached eggs or burritos.

ingredients

prep time: 10 minutes | *yields:* 4 servings

2 medium-size red tomatoes, seeded and diced

½ red onion, minced

1 jalapeño, minced

¼ cup chopped cilantro

½ teaspoon kosher salt

variations

Try freshly squeezed lemon or lime juice. Add a minced mango. Use a shallot or sweet onion for a less pungent flavor. Add a clove of minced garlic for more bite.

Combine all the ingredients in a small mixing bowl, and store in an airtight container for up to 5 days.

hummus and pita

Hummus is seductively garlicky, tangy, and creamy all at the same time. The best version I've ever tasted came from a natural foods store in Portland, Oregon, that's sadly no longer in business. I think I've finally recreated the perfect balance of flavors with this recipe. We usually make a batch on Monday nights and have it for the rest of the week. It's great with pita, but also with pretzels or crudités. Spread it on sandwiches stuffed with grilled vegetables or lamb.

prep time: 10 minutes | *cooking time:* 5 minutes | *yields:* 4 servings

Preheat the oven to 325 degrees. Wrap the pitas in aluminum foil and place in the oven to warm.

Drain the garbanzo beans, reserving 2 tablespoons of the liquid. Place the garbanzo beans, tahini, garlic, lemon juice, salt, and pepper in a food processor and blend until smooth. With the machine running, slowly pour in the olive oil until incorporated. If the hummus seems too thick, drizzle in just enough of the reserved bean liquid until thinned to the preferred consistency.

Spoon the hummus onto the red cabbage leaves. Garnish with parsley and paprika, and lightly drizzle with more olive oil, if desired. Serve with the warmed pitas.

ingredients

- 4 pitas
- 1 (15-ounce) can garbanzo beans
- ¼ cup tahini
- 1 clove garlic
- 3 tablespoons freshly squeezed lemon juice (about 1 medium lemon)
- 1 teaspoon kosher salt
- Pinch of freshly ground black pepper
- ½ cup extra-virgin olive oil, plus more for drizzling
- 2 sturdy red cabbage leaves for presentation
- Chopped fresh flat-leaf parsley for garnish
- Paprika for garnish

variations

Add 2 tablespoons of fresh herbs like mint or cilantro. Purée with roasted red peppers and walnuts for extra flavor. For a classic Italian dip, use white beans and fresh thyme instead of garbanzos and tahini.

pan-fried gruyère cheese

All men I know love bread and cheese. But then, who doesn't? This is my version of the Greek dish known as saganaki, which is usually made with kasseri or feta. I prefer Gruyère; it isn't as salty and punchy as feta, but has a rich, nutty flavor. When you really want to impress each other, serve flaming saganaki and flambé the cheese with a bit of brandy or ouzo.

prep time: 10 minutes | *cooking time:* 5 minutes | *yields:* 4 servings

Heat the oil in a large, nonstick sauté pan over medium-high heat.

Dip the slices of cheese in the beaten egg. Dredge in the flour until lightly coated on all sides, shaking off any excess. When the oil is hot, gently add the cheese to the pan and brown for 2 minutes on each side, or until light-golden brown.

Drain the fried cheese briefly on a paper towel to absorb any excess oil, and then immediately transfer the slices to a small serving dish. Spritz with lemon and garnish with parsley. Serve hot with Crostini (see below) or crackers.

ingredients

- 2 tablespoons canola oil
- 4 ounces Gruyère cheese, cut into ½-inch-thick slices
- 1 large egg, beaten
- ¼ cup all-purpose flour
- Lemon wedges for spritzing
- 1 tablespoon chopped fresh flat-leaf parsley for garnish

variations

Any hard or semi-hard cheese will work—Parmesan, Swiss, feta.

crostini

When store-bought crackers look just too, well, store-bought, these homemade toasts will provide the crunchy base you need for your appetizers. Day-old bread works just as well, if not better.

prep time: 5 minutes | *cooking time:* 10 minutes | *yields:* up to 60 crostini

Preheat the oven to 350 degrees. Cut the baguette into as many ½-inch-thick slices as you need. Brush both sides of bread slices lightly with olive oil and place on a baking sheet. Sprinkle the slices with salt. Bake for 8 to 10 minutes, or until golden-brown and slightly crispy. Rub the toasted bread with the cut side of a garlic clove, if desired.

ingredients

French or sourdough baguette

Extra-virgin olive oil

Kosher salt to taste

Garlic cloves, cut in half (optional)

variations

Cut small squares of artisanal loaves instead of baguette rounds.

gingered chicken gyoza with green onion ponzu sauce

You can stop buying frozen gyoza (also called pot stickers) right now. They're not difficult to make from scratch, especially using store-bought dim sum wrappers. The dumplings taste delicious served hot or at room temperature and are easily frozen for later. Pop them out a few at a time for a quick last-minute appetizer—they don't even need thawing first. The dipping sauce is extremely flexible if you want to change the flavor. I love using sriracha, a spicy chile sauce with garlic.

prep time: 20 minutes | cooking time: 4 minutes | yields: 20 gyoza

To make the ponzu sauce, combine all the ingredients in a small bowl, stirring until the sugar is dissolved.

For the gyoza, bring a medium pot of water to boil over high heat. Blanch the cabbage for 2 minutes, or until just softened. Drain and set aside to cool.

Combine the onion, sesame seeds, sriracha, ginger, garlic, soy sauce, and salt in a medium bowl, and stir to combine. Add the ground chicken and blanched cabbage, and stir until just combined.

To make the gyoza, place a teaspoon of the chicken mixture in the center of each dim sum wrapper. Dampen one side of the wrapper with some water. Fold the wrapper over and press both sides together to make a seal, being careful to press out any air bubbles. (Freeze any of the dumplings you're not planning to cook immediately. Set them on a wax-paper lined baking sheet in a single layer. Once frozen, transfer the gyoza to a heavy-duty, resealable plastic bag and store in the freezer until ready to cook. You can prepare them straight from the freezer; simply add 2 to 3 minutes to the steaming time.)

Set a large skillet over medium-high heat and add the canola oil. When the oil is hot, add the gyoza, in batches if necessary, and cook for two minutes on each side until lightly browned. Add a tablespoon of water to the pan, cover, and cook for an additional minute to steam slightly and finish cooking the meat. Remove the gyoza and place on paper towels to drain. Serve immediately with the Green Onion Ponzu Sauce and your favorite hot mustard.

ingredients

ponzu sauce

2 tablespoons seasoned rice vinegar

2 tablespoons soy sauce

2 tablespoons freshly squeezed lemon juice (1 small lemon)

½ jalapeño, minced

1 clove garlic, minced

1 teaspoon sugar

1 green onion, chopped

gyoza

2 cups shredded napa cabbage

1 green onion, finely chopped

¼ teaspoon sesame seeds, toasted

¼ teaspoon sriracha, or more to taste

1 teaspoon grated fresh ginger

1 clove garlic, minced

1 tablespoon soy sauce

¼ teaspoon kosher salt

½ pound ground chicken breast

20 round dim sum wrappers

3 tablespoons canola oil

Hot mustard for dipping

variations

Use ground pork instead of the chicken for a meatier flavor or minced bay shrimp for a lighter flavor.

truffled popcorn

Humble popcorn is utterly transformed by the intoxicating aroma of truffle oil. If you've never cooked with truffles, now's your chance to splurge on a decadent snack. Truffle oil can be hard to find and expensive, so you can buy an olive oil-truffle blend. If price is no object, buy a fresh truffle and grate a tiny bit onto the popcorn. Heaven. You may not even want to bother with the movie.

prep time: 10 minutes │ *cooking time:* 8 minutes │ *yields:* 4 cups popped

To pop the popcorn, place a Dutch oven or other large, heavy, lidded pot over medium-high heat. Add the oil and the popcorn. Twirl to coat the bottom of the pan evenly with the oil and the popcorn. Cover and cook, shaking the pan frequently and lifting the lid occasionally to let the steam escape, keeping your popcorn crisp.

When the popping almost stops, remove from the heat and pour the popcorn into a large bowl. Drizzle with the melted butter and truffle oil. Sprinkle with the Parmesan and salt. Toss well to distribute evenly.

ingredients

1½ tablespoons vegetable oil

3 to 4 tablespoons popping corn

2 tablespoons unsalted butter, melted

1 teaspoon truffle oil

⅓ cup finely grated Parmesan cheese

¼ teaspoon kosher salt

variations

Add chopped parsley for a bright, clean flavor. Grate with fresh nutmeg using a Microplane grater.

fresh shrimp rolls
with peanut-lime dipping sauce

A gem of Vietnamese restaurants is the fresh spring roll, a much lighter, fresher version of deep-fried egg rolls. They are truly simple to assemble at home. You can buy rice-paper wrappers, different from egg roll wrappers, and cellophane noodles at most grocery stores or at Asian markets. It can be tricky working with the sticky rice-paper wrappers. My solution is to spread out the softened rice paper on a damp towel—not a smooth plate or counter where it will stick.

ingredients

prep time: 20 minutes | *yields:* 4 servings

spring rolls

8 rice-paper wrappers

16 medium (31- to 35-count) shrimp, peeled, deveined, and cooked

1 head green leaf lettuce, whole leaves washed and dried

1 package cellophane noodles, cooked according to package directions

1 bunch mint, stems discarded and leaves chopped

1 bunch cilantro, chopped

dipping sauce

¼ cup soy sauce

1 tablespoon peanut butter

1 tablespoon freshly squeezed lime juice (about 1 medium lime)

variations

Diced baked tofu or cooked crab make a delicious alternative to the shrimp.

To make the spring rolls, fill a medium saucepan halfway with water. Set over high heat and bring to a boil, and then turn off the heat. Prepare all the ingredients to make assembly easy, and place a dampened kitchen towel on your workspace.

Working with one wrapper at a time, dip the wrapper in the hot water for a few seconds to soften. Remove and place the wrapper on the dampened kitchen towel. Place 2 shrimp vertically down the center of the wrapper. (The pink shrimp will show through the translucent wrapper to beautiful effect.) Place a leaf of lettuce and one-eighth of the noodles, mint, and cilantro on top of the shrimp and down the center of the wrapper. Fold the two ends inward, and roll up the wrapper like a burrito. Press the edge of the wrapper to seal, and place the finished roll on a serving dish, shrimp-side up. Repeat the same process for the remaining rolls, and cover with a damp towel to keep them moist as you work.

To make the dipping sauce, whisk together the soy sauce, peanut butter, and lime juice in a small bowl. Serve the rolls and dipping sauce immediately or store in the refrigerator for up to 30 minutes.

asian ground turkey lettuce cups

There is something very intimate about eating with your hands, isn't there? For this cool, refreshing appetizer, simply tear off pieces of lettuce and fill them with the turkey mixture, as you would a soft taco. The recipe calls for a lot of ingredients, but after you've purchased them the first time, you'll have your Asian pantry pretty well stocked. We make this dish once a week and never tire of it. Serve this meal with any long-grain white rice. I prefer Basmati.

ingredients

prep time: 20 minutes | *cooking time:* 15 minutes | *yields:* 4 servings

- 2 tablespoons canola oil
- 1 medium-size white onion, diced
- 3 tablespoons minced fresh ginger
- 2 tablespoons minced fresh garlic
- 1½ cups diced button mushrooms
- 1 (8-ounce) can water chestnuts, drained and diced
- 1 pound ground turkey
- Kosher salt and freshly ground black pepper to taste
- 1 tablespoon sesame oil
- 2 tablespoons seasoned rice vinegar
- 1 teaspoon fish sauce
- 1 teaspoon soy sauce
- 1 tablespoon hot mustard
- 1 tablespoon hoisin sauce
- 1 tablespoon black bean sauce
- 1 teaspoon Worcestershire sauce
- 1 teaspoon sriracha (see page 27)
- 1 teaspoon sesame seeds
- 1 bunch cilantro, minced
- 1 green onion, sliced
- 1 head of romaine or butter lettuce, washed and dried

variations

Substitute ground pork or chicken for the turkey, and basil or flat-leaf parsley for the cilantro.

To make the turkey filling, set a large, heavy sauté pan or wok over medium heat. Add the canola oil. Add the onion, and sauté for 2 minutes until translucent. Add the ginger and garlic, and sauté for 1 minute. Add the mushrooms and water chestnuts, and sauté for another 2 minutes. Add the turkey, season with salt and pepper, and sauté until the turkey is cooked through.

Add the sesame oil, rice vinegar, fish sauce, soy sauce, hot mustard, hoisin, black bean sauce, Worcestershire, sriracha, and sesame seeds. Stir thoroughly to distribute flavors, sautéing for 2 minutes. Remove from the heat and add the cilantro and green onion.

Serve with lettuce leaves to use as serving "cups" or wrappers.

cayenne onion rings

Who doesn't like piping-hot, just-fried onion rings? These crunchy rings will slide in perfectly to a meal of French Dip Sandwiches (page 119) or the Pan-Seared Rib-Eye (page 91). The cayenne gives the onion rings a sophisticated flavor. Feel free to experiment by dipping broccoli, mushrooms, zucchini, or dill pickles in the batter for a fried veggie frenzy.

prep time: 10 minutes | *cooking time:* 25 minutes | *yields:* 4 servings

Preheat the oven to 225 degrees. Line a baking sheet with several layers of paper towels and set aside.

Combine 1 cup of flour with the baking soda, salt, and cayenne in a large bowl. Stir well to combine. Add the ginger ale and eggs, and whisk until the batter is smooth.

Separate the onion slices into individual rings. Pat the rings dry and place in a medium mixing bowl. Sprinkle with the remaining flour and toss to coat.

Pour enough oil to come one-third of the way up a deep, heavy saucepan, and set over medium-high heat. Sprinkle drops of the batter in the oil to test. When the oil begins to sizzle (about 350 degrees), quickly prepare the rings for frying.

Working in batches, shake off any excess flour and dip the rings into the batter. Place directly into the hot oil with tongs and fry about 4 minutes per batch until they are golden brown and float to the surface. Gently remove the fried rings from the oil with tongs or a spider and drain on the paper towels. Set the drained rings on a wire rack and set in the warm oven until all the batches are completed and ready to serve, up to 20 minutes in advance. Season with additional salt and cayenne to taste.

ingredients

- 1 cup plus 2 tablespoons all-purpose flour, divided
- ½ teaspoon baking soda
- 1 teaspoon kosher salt, plus more to taste
- ¼ teaspoon cayenne pepper, or more to taste
- ⅔ cup ginger ale
- 2 large eggs
- Canola or vegetable oil for frying
- 1 large onion, sliced into ⅛-inch-thick rings

variations

Use beer instead of ginger ale.

Double- and triple-dip the onion slices for an extra-thick batter.

Up the cayenne for a spicier kick.

kalamata olive tapenade

Take the time to chop the ingredients instead of using a food processor. You'll get very distinct, chunky flavors instead of a paste. (That's the beauty of cooking with a partner: You can divide up the work, and it'll go twice as fast.) Increase or decrease the ingredients for different flavors. If you love capers, add more! Hate anchovies? Leave them out. There's plenty of wiggle room here—I first tried this recipe in cooking school, and it has evolved ever since. Try your handmade tapenade on a sandwich with grilled vegetables.

ingredients

6½ ounces Kalamata olives, pitted (about 1 cup)

1 tablespoon capers, rinsed

1 ounce unsalted whole almonds (about 20 almonds)

1 clove garlic

2 tablespoons chopped fresh basil

½ teaspoon freshly grated lemon zest, plus more for garnish

¼ teaspoon anchovy paste

2 tablespoons extra-virgin olive oil

¼ teaspoon freshly ground black pepper

variations

Mix different types of olives; try walnuts or pine nuts for a change.

prep time: 15 minutes | *yields:* 4 servings

With a very sharp knife, finely chop the olives, capers, almonds, and garlic to roughly the same size. Place in a small bowl and add the basil, lemon zest, anchovy paste, olive oil, and pepper. Stir to combine and let stand at room temperature for the flavors to meld.

Garnish with peels of lemon zest, and serve with Crostini (page 25) or endive for dipping. For a complete appetizer, serve alongside the Antipasto Platter below.

antipasto platter

ingredients

8 thin slices salami

4 slices prosciutto, cut in half

1 cucumber, sliced

3 plum tomatoes, cut into wedges

8 ounces fresh buffalo mozzarella, sliced

variations

Add roasted red pepper slices and marinated artichoke hearts.

prep time: 10 minutes | *yields:* 4 servings

Arrange all the ingredients attractively on a platter. Serve with the Kalamata Olive Tapenade (see above) and Crostini (page 25) or thin Italian breadsticks.

chapter two salads

Let's be honest: salad is never going to be as exciting as the main course. And not every day of a relationship is as much fun as New Year's Eve and the Fourth of July rolled into one. But salads can help us appreciate everyday joys like the sweetness of a perfectly ripe tomato, the saltiness of crisp-fried bacon, and the cool crunch of lettuce. And maybe, after a while, when you've really gotten good at appreciating the little things, a plate full of French Potato Salad will seem like a perfectly good lunch all on its own. Maybe sometimes a Baby Spinach Salad, heaped with avocado, bacon, and Swiss cheese, is all you really need for dinner. Just a big salad and your sweetheart's company.

master vinaigrette dressing

This dressing, made often enough, will come more naturally to you than using anything bottled. It can be easily flavored to complement any main course you're serving. Whisking it together yourself is part of the fun, but you can use a food processor or immersion blender for a more emulsified result.

ingredients

- 1 teaspoon Dijon mustard
- ⅛ teaspoon sugar
- ¼ teaspoon kosher salt
- ⅛ teaspoon freshly ground black pepper
- 1½ tablespoons Champagne or sherry vinegar
- ¼ cup extra-virgin olive oil

variations

Use a white balsamic vinegar for a sweeter dressing, or if you like it tart, use the juice from half a lemon.

prep time: 2 minutes | *yields:* ⅓ cup

Whisk together the mustard, sugar, salt, pepper, and vinegar in a medium bowl. Gradually whisk in the olive oil in a slow, steady stream until the mixture is creamy.

Alternatively, make a large batch by doubling or tripling the recipe and prepare in a mini food processor. Or place all the ingredients in a glass jar or storage container, and use an immersion blender or shake by hand to thoroughly combine. Cover well and store in the refrigerator for up to 1 week. Shake well before using.

asian cucumber salad

This cool salad goes well with the Sesame-Crusted Ahi (page 21), but it's perfect for any warm summer evening. Cutting long, paper-thin slices of cucumber with a sharp vegetable peeler gives an elegant look to the salad, but you can certainly slice or dice the cucumber for a less formal presentation.

ingredients

- 1 cup seasoned rice vinegar
- ½ teaspoon granulated sugar
- 1 tablespoon minced red bell pepper
- ¼ teaspoon black or white sesame seeds
- 1 medium shallot, finely diced
- 1 cucumber, peeled

variations

Add chopped roasted peanuts or cashews after chilling for a more robust flavor and a bit of crunch.

prep time: 5 minutes | *chilling time:* 30 minutes | *yields:* 2 servings

Whisk together the rice vinegar, sugar, bell pepper, sesame seeds, and shallot in a mixing bowl. Using a sharp vegetable peeler, shave the cucumber into long, thin ribbons. Toss gently in the dressing. Cover and chill for 30 minutes. Let stand at room temperature for 5 minutes before serving.

roasted chicken salad with beets and gorgonzola

This salad pairs hand-pulled chicken with the earthy sweetness of roasted beets and salty cheese. Savor it in the winter or the summer by either roasting your own chicken and beets or buying rotisserie chicken and jarred beets. Pick up a loaf of sourdough bread and toast slices just before serving. If planning on leftovers, toss the lettuce separately from the remaining ingredients, which will keep well until the next day.

prep time: 15 minutes | *cooking time:* 1 hour | *yields:* 2 servings

Preheat the oven to 400 degrees. Cover a baking sheet with a piece of aluminum foil, and set the beets on the foil. Drizzle with the olive oil and sprinkle with kosher salt and pepper. Fold up the foil around the beets and roast in the oven until tender when tested with a knife, 45 minutes to an hour. Remove from the oven and let rest until cool enough to handle. Remove from the foil and peel the skin off with your fingers or rub off with a paper towel. (Careful what you wear—beets can stain most anything red. Latex gloves will keep your hands clean.) Slice the beets thinly.

Combine the lettuce, chicken, walnuts, blue cheese, and parsley together in a large bowl and toss with the Sherry Shallot Vinaigrette (page 55). Divide the salad between 2 plates, top with the sliced beets, and sprinkle with a twist of black pepper.

toasting nuts:

Set a small skillet over medium-low heat and add the nuts. Toast for about 2 minutes, tossing occasionally, until you begin to smell their nuttiness. (Watch carefully—they can change from nicely warmed and perfectly toasted to bitter and burned in a flash.) Remove the nuts immediately from the heat and let cool before chopping.

ingredients

- 2 medium-size red beets, scrubbed but not trimmed
- 1 tablespoon olive oil
- Kosher salt and freshly ground black pepper to taste
- 1 small head red leaf lettuce, washed, dried, and torn into bite-sized pieces
- 2 cups shredded roasted chicken
- ¼ cup chopped walnuts, toasted
- ¼ cup crumbled Gorgonzola or other blue cheese
- 4 sprigs flat-leaf parsley, stems discarded and leaves roughly chopped
- 3 tablespoons Sherry Shallot Vinaigrette, or more if desired (page 55)

variations

Try using pork tenderloin instead of chicken, and feta or goat cheese instead of blue. Stuff the salad into warmed pita pockets for sandwiches.

baby spinach salad with bacon and swiss

For this salad, I like to use baby spinach, which is sweeter and more tender than leaf spinach. Bacon transforms it from healthy and predictable into a bona fide treat.

ingredients

prep time: 15 minutes | *cooking time:* 6 minutes | *yields:* 4 servings

dressing

4 strips bacon

1½ tablespoons freshly squeezed lemon juice (about ½ medium lemon)

1 tablespoon Dijon mustard

1 teaspoon honey or brown sugar

Freshly ground black pepper to taste

Kosher salt to taste

Extra-virgin olive oil, as needed

salad

4 cups baby spinach, washed and dried

¼ cup grated Swiss cheese

½ avocado, cubed

½ small red onion, finely chopped

variations

Add sautéed mushrooms.

Substitute ricotta salata, a slightly dry and salty cheese, for the Swiss, and crumble it in.

To make the dressing, set a medium sauté pan over medium heat and add the bacon. Cook, turning once or twice, until crispy. Drain on paper towels and crumble into bite-size pieces, reserving the rendered fat in the pan.

To make the dressing, add the lemon juice, mustard, honey, and several grinds of black pepper to the warm bacon fat and whisk until well combined. Dip a leaf of spinach into the dressing to taste. Add salt if needed and whisk in up to ¼ cup olive oil if the dressing seems too tart.

To assemble the salad, place the spinach, cheese, bacon, avocado, and onion in a large bowl. Drizzle with the dressing and toss to coat evenly. Place on serving plates and season with a bit of freshly ground pepper.

green garden salad

This salad's beauty is its simplicity and potential. Make it your own by adding vegetables at their peak from the farmers market. Have fun improvising together with whatever's in season and looks good.

ingredients

prep time: 5 minutes | *yields:* 4 servings

1 head Boston lettuce, washed and dried

2 tablespoons Master Vinaigrette (page 38), or more if needed

½ avocado, diced

¼ cup cherry tomatoes, cut in half

Freshly ground black pepper

variations

Sliced carrots, diced green pepper, sweet cooked corn, or steamed asparagus all make good additions.

Gently toss the lettuce with the dressing, adding more if needed. Place on serving plates, scatter with the avocado and tomato halves. Season with freshly ground pepper and serve immediately.

arugula with shaved parmesan and lemon vinaigrette

In every bite of this quick, easy salad you'll taste the rich, sharp flavor of Parmesan, the refreshing, peppery bitterness of arugula, and the bright acidity of lemon. A vegetable peeler will make quick work of the Parmesan, creating thin shards of nutty cheese. But my favorite utensil for grating is the Microplane, which came to market after a clever wife stole one of her husband's woodworking tools to use in the kitchen. (Now that's a great partnership!) Using the Microplane will change the texture of the cheese entirely, creating an airy, cloud-soft sprinkling of flavor.

prep time: 5 minutes | *yields:* 4 small salads

Combine the lemon juice, olive oil, salt, and pepper in a large mixing bowl. Whisk to combine. Add the arugula and toss to coat evenly with the dressing.

Place the dressed leaves in a serving bowl or on individual plates. Using a vegetable peeler, shave shards of Parmesan over the salad and add several more twists of pepper, if desired.

ingredients

1   tablespoon freshly squeezed lemon juice (½ small lemon)

3   tablespoons extra-virgin olive oil

Kosher salt and freshly ground black pepper to taste.

1   (6-ounce) bag arugula

Parmigiano-Reggiano for shaving

variations

Top with broiled or grilled salmon. Dress slices of smoked pork loin with this zingy salad and wrap in a warmed pita.

french potato salad with fennel

Fennel is extremely popular in other countries and is finally gaining much-due recognition here in the States. The creamy russet potatoes and tarragon create the perfect environment in which to highlight the unusual flavor of anise. The salad's sophisticated flavors will appeal to mature palates.

prep time: 15 minutes | *cooking & chilling:* 45 minutes | *yields:* 6-8 servings

Place the potatoes in a large pot of water and bring to a boil over high heat. Cook until the potatoes are soft but not mushy, about 15 minutes. Drain.

While the potatoes are cooking, whisk together the lemon juice, olive oil, salt, and pepper in a large bowl. Add the hot potatoes to the lemon juice mixture and stir to combine. Stir in the celery, fennel, and red onion. Cover and chill for 30 minutes, or until the potatoes are cold. Fold in the mayonnaise, fennel fronds, and tarragon.

ingredients

3 large russet potatoes, peeled and cut into 1-inch cubes

3 tablespoons freshly squeezed lemon juice (about 1 medium lemon)

3 tablespoons extra-virgin olive oil

½ teaspoon kosher salt

½ teaspoon freshly ground black pepper

2 stalks celery, diced

1 small fennel bulb, diced

1 small red onion, minced

⅓ cup mayonnaise

1 tablespoon chopped fennel fronds

2 tablespoons chopped fresh tarragon

variations

Garnish with a sliced hard-boiled egg and crumbled bits of bacon. For an American-style salad, replace the fennel bulb with ¼ cup diced dill pickles, and the fennel fronds with fresh dill.

heirloom tomato salad
with feta cheese and balsamic vinegar

In our garden, we have several varieties of tomatoes: plum, cherry, and heirlooms. Great tomatoes require very little adornment. Here I simply sprinkle them with a bit of salty cheese and drizzle them with aged balsamic vinegar and fruity olive oil. There isn't a better way to end the summer.

ingredients

prep time: 5 minutes | *yields:* 2-4 servings

- 3 medium-sized heirloom tomatoes
- 2 tablespoons crumbled feta cheese
- 1 tablespoon good-quality balsamic vinegar
- 1 tablespoon extra-virgin olive oil, or more to taste
- Kosher salt and freshly ground black pepper to taste
- Fresh basil leaves for garnish

variations

If you can't find heirloom tomatoes, use the beefsteak variety or grape tomatoes sliced in half.

Cut the tomatoes into ¼-inch slices. Arrange them on a plate, overlapping in a circle. Sprinkle with the feta and drizzle with the vinegar and olive oil. Season with salt and pepper, garnish with basil, and serve immediately.

caesar salad with sourdough croutons

Caesar salad is a classic, and this fantastically light and fresh version won't be too heavy to precede an entrée. Both parties should indulge in this salad, due to the garlicky nature of the creamy dressing. The flavors are only enhanced with a glass of dry white wine. Fair warning: the croutons are addictive. Try not to eat them all before the salad is served.

prep time: 20 minutes | *cooking time:* 5 minutes | *yields:* 4 servings

For the croutons, set a large sauté pan over medium heat and add the butter and olive oil. Add the bread and sprinkle with the herbes de Provence, salt, and pepper. Cook, turning occasionally, until crisp and golden brown on all sides.

To make the dressing, whisk together the garlic, anchovy paste, Parmesan, lemon juice, Worcestershire, dry mustard, and pepper in a large mixing bowl. Drizzle in the olive oil in a steady stream, whisking continuously until the dressing is emulsified. Taste, and add salt if needed. Pour half the dressing into a small pitcher to serve on the side.

To assemble the salad, add the lettuce and croutons to the remaining dressing and toss until evenly coated. Place on chilled salad plates and garnish with a lemon wedge. Serve immediately with extra dressing on the side.

ingredients

croutons

1 tablespoon unsalted butter

3 tablespoons olive oil

1½ cups cubed sourdough bread

¼ teaspoon herbes de Provence

Kosher salt and freshly ground black pepper to taste

dressing

1 teaspoon well-crushed garlic

1 teaspoon anchovy paste

⅓ cup freshly grated Parmesan cheese

3 tablespoons freshly squeezed lemon juice (about 1 medium lemon)

¼ teaspoon Worcestershire sauce

¼ teaspoon ground mustard

Freshly ground black pepper to taste

½ cup extra-virgin olive oil

Kosher salt to taste

salad

2 hearts of romaine, washed and dried

Lemon wedges for garnish

variations

Whisk a pasteurized egg yolk into the dressing for extra decadence. Top with grilled chicken, fish, or shrimp for a main course.

buttermilk blue cheese dressing

Making your own dressing at home is easier than you might think. This dressing is lighter, more versatile, and better-tasting than anything you'll find in the store. Adding ½ cup of sour cream turns it into a dip for Buffalo Chicken Satay (page 17) and crudités.

prep time: 5 minutes | *yields:* 1½ cups

Whisk all the ingredients together in a small mixing bowl until well combined. Crumble in more blue cheese for a thicker dressing.

ingredients

1 cup buttermilk

2 ounces blue cheese, or more if desired, crumbled

¼ cup mayonnaise

1 clove garlic, chopped

¼ teaspoon freshly ground black pepper

Pinch of kosher salt

variations

Use Greek yogurt instead of mayonnaise, and add chopped fresh herbs of your choice.

sherry shallot vinaigrette

This simple vinaigrette works well on any combination of mixed greens. The shallots give it a mild flavor that's much more subtle than you would get from raw onion or garlic.

prep time: 5 minutes | *yields:* 1 cup

Combine the shallot, Dijon, honey, vinegar, salt, and pepper in a mixing bowl. Slowly drizzle in the olive oil, whisking continuously until emulsified. Use immediately or store in the refrigerator for up to 3 days. Shake well before using.

ingredients

2 tablespoons minced shallot

1 teaspoon Dijon mustard

1 teaspoon honey

⅓ cup sherry vinegar

¼ teaspoon kosher salt

¼ teaspoon freshly ground black pepper

⅔ cup extra-virgin olive oil

variations

Try a walnut or hazelnut oil instead of fruity olive. Invest in aged sherry vinegar for exceptional flavor on everyday greens.

chapter two soups

Cooking together is an invitation to know each other better, even if you've been together forever. As you're stirring the tomato soup and putting together the grilled cheese sandwiches, you might share nearly forgotten childhood memories of eating that same meal, swapping stories about snow days, chicken pox, and first crushes. Every soup has an element like this. Eating gazpacho together says: *I love you and I love your garlic breath.* Making my Roasted Cauliflower Soup together lets your partner know: *I trust you. I've always hated cauliflower, but you swear this is going to be good and I believe you.*

thai chicken and lemongrass soup

We love Thai food, and we never tire of this soup. Each of the dozens of restaurants in Los Angeles's Thai Town has its own variation of this delectable soup. Try it at your local Thai joint and then try to make it better at home. To bruise lemongrass, gently crush the stem with the flat of a knife to release its flavors. If you can't find fresh stalks, look for tubes of lemongrass paste in the produce department and add a bit to the soup.

prep time: 10 minutes | *cooking time:* 30 minutes | *yields:* 6 servings

Set a Dutch oven or large saucepan over medium heat and add the oil. Sauté the onions until translucent and soft, 4 to 5 minutes. Add the bamboo shoots and sauté another 2 minutes. Add the chicken broth, fish sauce, lemongrass, and ginger. Simmer 15 minutes to let the flavors meld.

Add the chicken and let simmer 3 to 4 minutes, or until just cooked through. Stir in the coconut milk and lime juice, remove the lemongrass stalks, and serve hot.

ingredients

- 2 tablespoons canola oil
- 1 medium onion, thinly sliced
- ½ cup sliced bamboo shoots
- 6 cups low-sodium chicken broth
- 2 tablespoons fish sauce
- 2 stalks lemongrass, cut in half and bruised to release flavor
- 1 tablespoon finely minced fresh ginger
- 2 skinless, boneless chicken breasts, thinly sliced
- 1 can light coconut milk, shaken
  Juice of 1 medium lime

variations

For a spicier soup, experiment with whole or sliced Thai or serrano chiles, removing the seeds and the membranes. Add Jasmine rice for a complete meal.

french onion soup

French onion soup is salty and caramel-sweet with a deep, rich, beefy broth that will warm you to your core. This recipe calls for dry white wine, but you can substitute a dry red for a more traditional broth. For another presentation, serve the soup deconstructed. Strain the onions and place in the bottom of each bowl. Serve the hot broth from a teapot, pouring it over the onions at the table, and pass around cheese toasts. Trust me on the nutmeg and don't skip it: you've never had French Onion Soup like this.

ingredients

- 4 large yellow onions
- 4 tablespoons (½ stick) unsalted butter
- 2 sprigs thyme, plus more for garnish
- ½ teaspoon kosher salt
- 1 tablespoon all-purpose flour
- ½ cup dry white wine
- 1 (32-ounce) carton low-sodium beef broth (4 cups)
- ½ teaspoon freshly ground black pepper
- 8 baguette slices, toasted
- 4 ounces grated Gruyère or Emmental cheese
- 2 tablespoons freshly grated Parmesan cheese
- ¼ teaspoon freshly grated nutmeg, divided

variations

Add sautéed cremini mushrooms. Try Vidalia onions or Texas 1015s instead of yellow.

prep time: 15 minutes | *cooking time:* 80 minutes | *yields:* 4 servings

Cut the onions in half, stem to stem. Peel and thinly slice in half circles.

Set a large, heavy pot over medium-low heat and add the butter. When the butter melts, add the onions, thyme sprigs, and salt. Cook, stirring occasionally, until the onions are deep golden brown, about 45 minutes. (Take your time—quickly sautéing over high heat may turn the onions brown, but they'll taste burned, not caramelized like they do from long, slow cooking.)

Add the flour and cook, stirring constantly, for 1 minute. Stir in the wine and cook, stirring constantly, for 2 minutes. Stir in the broth and pepper. Increase the heat to high and bring to a boil. Reduce the heat and simmer for 30 minutes, stirring occasionally.

Preheat the broiler to high. Discard the thyme sprigs and divide the soup among 4 ovenproof bowls set on a baking sheet. Sprinkle with a pinch of the nutmeg. Float two toasted baguette slices in each soup bowl. Sprinkle with the Gruyère and Parmesan. Set the baking sheet about 6 inches under the broiler and broil until the cheese is golden and bubbly, about 2 minutes. Using pot holders, transfer each bowl onto serving plates. Sprinkle with the remaining nutmeg and garnish with fresh thyme.

homemade chicken noodle soup with fresh herbs

Because every once in a while we all love a quickie. This soup comes together in minutes but tastes like it's been stewing all day. You can add another meat like cooked, sliced Italian sausage to make it even more man-friendly.

ingredients

prep time: 15 minutes | *cooking time:* 45 minutes | *yields:* 6 servings

- 1 tablespoon olive oil
- 2 medium carrots, sliced into rounds
- 2 stalks celery, chopped
- 1 small onion, chopped
- 2 cloves garlic, minced
- 2 (32-ounce) cartons low-sodium chicken broth (8 cups)
- 1 whole roasted chicken, skin discarded, meat shredded and bones set aside
- 1 sprig thyme
- 1 sprig tarragon
- 3 sprigs flat-leaf parsley
- 12 ounces no-yolk wide egg noodles
- Kosher salt to taste
- Freshly ground black pepper to taste

variations

Use barley, wild rice, or orzo for a more rustic soup.

Heat the oil in a large soup pot over medium-high. Add the carrots, celery, and onion. Cook, stirring often, until softened, about 7 minutes. Add the garlic and cook for 2 more minutes. Add the chicken broth, bones, thyme, tarragon, and parsley and bring to a boil over high heat. Reduce the heat, cover, and simmer for 30 minutes. Skim any foam that comes to the top and discard.

Remove the bones and herb sprigs from the soup. If planning to serve all the soup immediately, add the noodles directly to the soup. Bring to a boil and cook until just shy of *al dente*. Add the shredded chicken and cook until just warmed through, 1 or 2 minutes. Taste and add salt and pepper if needed. Serve immediately with crackers or crusty warm bread.

If not planning to serve the soup immediately or all at once, cook the egg noodles separately in a large pot of boiling, salted water according to package directions. Drain and add the noodles to each bowl of soup to keep them from overcooking and becoming mushy.

minestrone

On cold winter days, my family would often make this Italian favorite, the "everything but the kitchen sink" of soups. Served with garlic bread, it makes a wonderfully satisfying first course or a light dinner. It will taste like humble comfort food and be even better if you splurge on good Parmigiano-Reggiano. Drop the rind of the cheese in the pot as the soup cooks. It will add an extra salty, cheesy layer of flavor.

prep time: 15 minutes | *cooking time:* 25 minutes | *yields:* 4 servings

Set a large saucepan over medium-high heat and add the oil. Add the onion and sauté until soft, about 5 minutes. Add the garlic and tomatoes, and cook 5 minutes more.

Stir in chicken broth, garbanzo beans, kidney beans, pasta, oregano, rosemary, and red pepper flakes. Bring to a boil, reduce the heat, and cover. Simmer 10 to 12 minutes, or until the pasta is just shy of *al dente*.

Add the escarole and cook for 2 minutes, or until it wilts. Season with salt and pepper, and garnish with large shavings of Parmesan.

ingredients

2 tablespoons olive oil

1 small onion, chopped

4 cloves garlic, finely chopped

3 medium tomatoes, diced

1 (32-ounce) carton low-sodium chicken broth (4 cups)

1 (15-ounce) can garbanzo beans, rinsed and drained

1 (15-ounce) can red kidney beans, rinsed and drained

⅓ cup dried pasta

1 teaspoon chopped fresh oregano

1 teaspoon chopped fresh rosemary

Pinch of red pepper flakes

1½ cups roughly chopped fresh escarole

Kosher salt and freshly ground black pepper to taste

Freshly shaved Parmesan cheese for garnish

variations

Use basil instead of the oregano and rosemary, add cooked sausage or chicken, or use white or black beans in place of the garbanzo and kidney beans.

roasted cauliflower soup

Don't be discouraged if your significant other doesn't like the sound of a healthy roasted cauliflower soup at first. Roasting yields its sweetness, and it's sinfully creamy without adding any cream.

prep time: 10 minutes | *cooking time:* 1 hour | *yields:* 4 servings

Preheat the oven to 350 degrees. Place the cauliflower florets, onion, and whole garlic cloves on a rimmed baking sheet. Drizzle with 3 tablespoons of the olive oil, and season with the salt, pepper, and herbes de Provence. Toss to combine, and then distribute in an even layer on the baking sheet. Roast for 40 minutes, turning occasionally, or until golden brown.

Set a Dutch oven or a large, heavy saucepan over medium heat. Add the remaining 2 tablespoons of olive oil. Sauté the chopped garlic for 1 minute. Add the roasted cauliflower, garlic, and onion, and stir in the chicken broth. Simmer for 15 minutes, or until the florets are completely tender.

Purée with an immersion blender or in batches in a food processor or blender, being careful of the hot liquid and steam. Garnish with chives and croutons.

ingredients

1 head cauliflower, cut into florets

1 medium onion, roughly chopped

4 cloves garlic plus 1 tablespoon chopped

5 tablespoons olive oil, divided

Pinch of kosher salt

¼ teaspoon freshly ground black pepper

1 tablespoon herbes de Provence

1 (32-ounce) carton low-sodium chicken broth (4 cups)

Minced chives for garnish

Sourdough Croutons for garnish (page 53)

variations

Use a homemade stock, vegetable or chicken. Stir in ¼ cup of cream after cooking for decadence.

creamy tomato soup with sourdough grilled cheese

Use the most flavorful tomatoes you can find for this soup. If you don't grow your own, try your farmers market first. You can serve the soup cold on hot days, without adding the cream. In the winter, make the soup with canned Italian plum tomatoes and share a gooey grilled cheese sandwich.

ingredients

prep time: 15 minutes | *cooking time:* 25 minutes | *yields:* 4 servings

tomato soup

2 tablespoons unsalted butter

½ cup chopped onion

¼ cup chopped carrot

¼ cup chopped celery

4 large ripe tomatoes, chopped, or 1 (28-ounce) can whole tomatoes

1½ cups homemade or low-sodium chicken broth

½ cup heavy cream

Crème fraîche for garnish

grilled cheese

4 thin slices whole wheat or sourdough bread

2 sandwich-size slices Havarti cheese

2 sandwich-size slices extra-sharp Cheddar cheese

1½ tablespoons unsalted butter, divided

variations

Flavor your crème fraîche by blending it with a little roasted garlic, fresh herbs, or lemon juice. Add several slices of bacon, tomato, or avocado to the sandwich before grilling. Use Pepper Jack for a spicier sandwich.

To make the soup, set a medium, heavy-bottomed saucepan over medium heat and add the butter. When the butter melts, add the onions and sauté for 2 minutes. Add the carrots and celery and sauté for 5 minutes more. Add the tomatoes and chicken broth. Bring to a boil, reduce the heat, and simmer until the carrots are cooked through, 7 to 10 minutes.

Purée the vegetables with an immersion blender or in batches in a food processor or blender, being careful of the hot liquid and steam. Return the soup to the pan and stir in the cream. Set over medium-low heat until warmed through.

While the soup is warming, prepare the grilled cheese. For each sandwich, place one slice of Havarti and one slice of Cheddar between two pieces of bread. Set a large, nonstick skillet over medium heat and add half of the butter. When the butter melts, swirl to coat the pan and add the sandwiches. Cover and let cook about 4 minutes, or until golden-brown on the bottom. Lift the sandwiches from the pan with a spatula and add the remaining butter, if necessary. Swirl to coat the pan and add the sandwiches on the flip side. Cook, uncovered, until golden brown and crisp on the bottom. Remove from the pan and cut each sandwich in half.

Pour the soup into bowls, garnish with a spoon of crème fraîche, and serve with a grilled cheese half.

gazpacho

This chilled summer soup is as crisp and exciting as a midnight skinny dip. Use the freshest, ripest, most fragrant tomatoes you can buy and serve with garlic breadsticks, croutons, or vegetable crudités.

ingredients

prep time: 10 minutes | *yields:* 4 servings

- 2 medium-size ripe tomatoes
- 1 small cucumber, peeled and seeded
- 1 red bell pepper, stemmed and seeded
- 1 small sweet onion
- 1 serrano chile, stemmed and seeded (optional)
- 1 clove garlic
- 1½ cups low-sodium chicken broth
- ½ cup tomato juice
- 1 tablespoon extra-virgin olive oil
- 1 tablespoon red wine vinegar
- Kosher salt and freshly ground black pepper to taste
- Lime wedges for garnish

variations

Serve in a shot glass for a refreshing amuse bouche or light appetizer.

Try fresh herbs instead of the chile.

Blend in several slices of overripe cantaloupe in place of the pepper, onion, chile, and garlic for a sweet soup.

Roughly chop the tomatoes, cucumber, bell pepper, onion, serrano chile (if using), and garlic. Place in the bowl of a food processor and purée to the desired degree of smoothness. (Purée in batches if necessary.) Add the chicken broth, tomato juice, olive oil, and red wine vinegar and pulse to incorporate.

Taste and add salt and pepper as needed. The soup can be made up to a day in advance and stored in the refrigerator. Pour into small bowls and garnish with a wedge of lime.

cream of mushroom soup

There is canned cream of mushroom soup, and there is cream of mushroom soup. It's like the difference between a CZ and that antique asher-cut you've been eyeing. A bag of Funyuns and beer-battered, triple-dipped onion rings. A 49-cent waxy candy bar and a melt-in-your mouth artisanal chocolate. There's a time for canned mushroom soup—like when you're making green bean casserole for a potluck you don't want to attend—and there's a time for homemade, rich-beyond-belief creamy mushroom soup. That time is, most decidedly, date night.

prep time: 20 minutes | *cooking time:* 30 minutes | *yields:* 4-6 servings

ingredients

- 3 tablespoons unsalted butter
- 1 tablespoon olive oil
- 1 medium-size yellow onion, chopped
- 2 cloves garlic, minced
- 1 teaspoon chopped fresh thyme or ½ teaspoon dried
- 12 ounces cremini mushrooms, sliced
- 8 ounces button mushrooms, sliced
- ¼ cup all-purpose flour
- 1 (32-ounce) carton low-sodium chicken broth (4 cups)
- 2 cups whole milk
- ½ teaspoon freshly ground black pepper
- Kosher salt to taste
- Minced chives for garnish

Set a large saucepan over medium heat and add the butter and olive oil. When the butter melts, add the onion, garlic, and thyme and sauté 2 minutes, or until the onions are translucent. Add the mushrooms and sauté about 5 minutes, or until the mushrooms have released their liquid. Add the flour and sauté another 1 to 2 minutes.

Whisk in the chicken broth, bring to a simmer, and let cook 10 minutes. Whisk in the milk and simmer for 10 more minutes.

Using an immersion blender, blend to the desired degree of smoothness. (Alternatively, puree in the blender, being careful of the hot steam.) Season with salt and pepper, and sprinkle with snipped chives. Serve with crusty, buttered bread.

variations

Add a few tablespoons of sherry or Madeira. Go wild with mushrooms like trumpets, shitakes, chanterelles, hedgehogs, or morels. Keep it chunky for a substantial-tasting soup. Make it silky by straining through a sieve.

tortilla soup

When you're in the mood for something sassy and spicy, try this Mexican tortilla soup. Mild ancho chiles, the dried version of fresh poblanos, give it a subtle kick that will leave your date begging for more. Just be sure to use a high-quality, low-sodium chicken broth—or make your own.

ingredients

prep time: 15 minutes | *cooking and soaking:* 70 minutes | *yields:* 4 servings

½ medium-size white onion, quartered

4 plum tomatoes, cut in half

2 cloves garlic

1 whole ancho chile

Peanut or vegetable oil for frying

3 corn tortillas, sliced into thin strips

½ teaspoon cumin

1 (32-ounce) carton low-sodium chicken broth (4 cups)

1 sprig oregano

Kosher salt to taste

2 green onions, thinly sliced for garnish

½ medium avocado, diced for garnish

Cilantro sprigs for garnish

1 jalapeño, sliced for garnish

1 lime, quartered for garnish

variations

Add shredded chicken or roasted pork shoulder to make this soup heartier fare. Grate in ¼ teaspoon of fresh nutmeg. Try vegetable or mushroom broth for a vegetarian dish. Add another dried ancho for a smokier soup.

Preheat the oven to 425 degrees. Place the onion, tomatoes, and garlic in a shallow baking dish and roast until the onion is lightly charred, about 20 minutes.

While the vegetables are roasting, remove the stem, seeds, and ribs from the ancho chile. Set a small, heavy skillet over medium heat. Add the chile and toast for a few seconds on each side to soften, or just until you start to smell the chile. Place the toasted chile in a small bowl and cover with hot water to reconstitute. Soak for 20 minutes, and then remove and pat dry.

Set a small, deep saucepan over medium heat and pour enough oil to come 1 inch up the sides. Place some paper towels on your workspace for draining the finished tortilla strips. Pinch off a small piece of corn tortilla and drop in the oil to test. When the oil begins to sizzle (about 350 degrees), add the remaining tortilla strips and fry until crispy, about 2 minutes. Fry in batches if the pan seems crowded. Drain on the paper towels.

Place the onion, tomatoes, garlic, chile, half the tortilla strips, and the cumin in the bowl of a food processor and purée until smooth.

Combine the chicken broth and chile purée in a medium saucepan over high heat. Bring to a boil, reduce the heat, and stir in the oregano. Simmer, stirring occasionally, until the soup has thickened slightly, 20 to 30 minutes. Taste and add salt if needed. Remove the oregano sprig and spoon the soup into bowls. Garnish with the remaining tortilla strips, the green onions, avocados, cilantro, jalapeño, and lime.

potato leek soup

This classic French soup traditionally does not have any herbs or spices beyond the basic salt and black pepper. The addition of tarragon and sage gives it a fresh herbal aroma. Serve it cold, and it becomes vichyssoise, a delicious example of understated elegance.

prep time: 15 minutes | *cooking time:* 30 minutes | *yields:* 4 servings

Set a large, heavy saucepan over medium-low heat and add the butter. Add the leeks, season with the salt and pepper, and cook for about 7 minutes, or until the leeks are soft. Stir in the broth and potatoes and bring to a boil over high heat. Reduce the heat, cover, and simmer for 20 minutes, or until the potatoes are soft.

While the potatoes are cooking, set a small saucepan over medium heat and arrange some paper towels on your workspace for draining the fried sage leaves. Pour enough vegetable oil in the saucepan to come ½ inch up the sides and set over medium-high heat. When the oil is hot, but not smoking (about 350 degrees), add the sage leaves and cook for a few seconds until crisp. Drain the crisped leaves on the paper towels.

Purée the potatoes and their cooking liquid with an immersion blender or in batches in a food processor or blender, being careful of the hot liquid and steam. Blend until smooth. Taste and season the soup with more salt and pepper if needed. Stir in the tarragon and garnish with the fried sage leaves.

ingredients

- 1½ tablespoons unsalted butter
- 2 large leeks, white and light green parts only, thinly sliced
- ¼ teaspoon kosher salt
- ⅛ teaspoon freshly ground black pepper
- 2½ cups low-sodium chicken broth
- 1 pound red or white potatoes, peeled and diced
- Vegetable oil for frying
- 8 fresh sage leaves for garnish
- 2 tablespoons finely chopped fresh tarragon

variations

Add either a pinch of nutmeg or a pinch of cayenne. Add a tablespoon of a different herb to change the flavor. Garnish with thinly sliced, crispy-fried leeks.

chapter four **entrées**

This is where we get to the meat and potatoes —of the meal and of the relationship. My recipes aren't necessarily hard work, but they take more effort than microwaving a Hot Pocket. Committing to an evening of chopping onions and rolling meatballs means you're serious about dinner and about your sweetie. You can get Pasta Bolognese at any Italian restaurant, so why bother making it at home? Because it's fun, that's why. This is the "quality time" you're always saying you need to spend together. Cooperating, communicating, working in sync, you are a perfect team! Stirring the sauce, adjusting the seasonings, licking each other's spoons…these are the good times.

angry shrimp pasta

The Italian word arrabbiata, *meaning "angry," refers to a variety of spicy dishes. Here, red pepper flakes give the shrimp a vigorous, "angry" kick. You can use any pasta you have on hand, and frozen, deveined shrimp work well—simply rinse the shrimp under cold running water until thawed. You'll love how quickly this dish comes together for a stress-free, weeknight dinner.*

prep time: 10 minutes | *cooking time:* 15 minutes | *yields:* 4 servings

Bring a large pot of salted water to a boil and cook the pasta according to package directions until *al dente*. Drain and toss with the 2 tablespoons of olive oil. Place in a serving bowl and cover to keep warm.

Set a large sauté pan over medium heat and add the remaining olive oil. Sprinkle in the red pepper flakes and garlic. Sauté until fragrant, being careful not to burn the garlic, about 1 minute.

Add the shrimp to the pan and cook about 1 minute per side, or until pink and just cooked through. Season with salt and pepper. Add the shrimp mixture to the pasta and sprinkle with the cilantro. Toss to combine. Serve with sliced lemon wedges and plenty of fresh, crusty bread.

ingredients

- 1 pound linguini, spaghetti, or penne pasta
- 2 tablespoons plus ¼ cup extra-virgin olive oil
- 1 teaspoon red pepper flakes
- 3 cloves garlic, minced
- 1 pound large shrimp, peeled and deveined
  Kosher salt and freshly ground black pepper
- 2 tablespoons minced cilantro
- 1 small lemon, cut into wedges

variations

Use roasted garlic instead of raw. Toss several large handfuls of baby spinach into the hot pasta and shrimp after cooking, and stir until the spinach wilts.

chicken chilaquile casserole

Chilaquiles are always very satisfying when made the traditional way—with not much more than tortillas, onions, tomatoes, garlic, and cheese—but here I have beefed up the original recipe to become an even heartier dish. With the addition of chicken, cream, and a few other ingredients, it becomes a substantial entrée, but it's still great reheated for a lazy, late-morning weekend breakfast with eggs on the side. Cotija is a crumbly white Mexican cheese with a salty flavor similar to, but even saltier than, feta.

ingredients

- 2 jalapeños, or more to taste
- 1 bunch cilantro, large stems removed
- 2 cloves garlic
- 1 medium onion, coarsely chopped
- 1 (7-ounce) can fire-roasted green chiles
  Kosher salt to taste
  Vegetable oil or shortening for greasing
- 12 corn tortillas, sliced into 1-inch strips
- ½ cup half-and-half
- 1 pound cooked chicken, shredded
- 12 ounces cotija cheese, crumbled
- 8 ounces Monterey Jack cheese, grated
- 2 green onions, thinly sliced for garnish
- 1 to 2 medium tomatoes, seeded and chopped for garnish
  Sour cream for garnish

variations

Replace the cotija with Monterey Jack, Pepper Jack, or mozzarella cheese.

prep time: 35 minutes | *cooking time:* 50 minutes | *yields:* 6 servings

Preheat the oven to 450 degrees. Place the jalapeños directly on a rack in the oven with a sheet pan placed on the rack below. Roast for 15 minutes, or until the skin begins to char. Place the charred pepper in a plastic or paper bag, seal, and let steam for 5 to 10 minutes.

Reduce the oven to 375 degrees. Wearing rubber or latex gloves, rub away the blackened skin from the pepper with your hands or scrape away with a knife—it's okay if a few charred bits remain. Slice in half, and discard the seeds, core, and membrane from the pepper.

Place the roasted jalapeños in the bowl of a food processor. Add the cilantro, garlic, onion, green chiles, and salt. Pulse until the mixture is finely chopped.

Grease an 11 x 7 x 2-inch casserole dish with vegetable oil. Place half of the tortilla strips in the bottom of the casserole dish. Pour the half-and-half over the tortilla strips. Spoon half of the cilantro mixture over the tortilla strips and distribute evenly. Top with half of the chicken, cotija, and Monterey Jack. Layer the remaining tortilla strips on top of the cheese. Top with the remaining cilantro mixture, chicken, cotija, and Monterey Jack.

Place on a middle rack in the oven and bake for 30 minutes, or until golden brown and and bubbly. Garnish with sliced green onions, fresh chopped tomatoes, and a dollop of sour cream before serving.

chicken paillard
with parmesan and lemon

To create this lighter version of Chicken Parmesan, I use Japanese panko—a big, flaky kind of breadcrumb—to create a perfectly crispy, crunchy, golden crust. If you can't find panko, you can make your own very coarse breadcrumbs by pulsing some stale bread in a food processor and then toasting it briefly.

prep time: 20 minutes | *cooking time:* 8 minutes | *yields:* 2 servings

Rinse the chicken breasts, place on a large sheet of plastic wrap, and cover with another sheet of plastic wrap. Pound the chicken to an even thickness with a meat pounder or heavy skillet. Remove from the plastic wrap and pat dry.

Place the flour on a plate and generously season with salt and pepper. Beat the eggs in a shallow bowl. Combine the panko and Parmesan on a plate.

Set a large sauté pan over medium-high heat. Add the oil. Dredge the chicken in the flour, shaking off any excess. Dip the chicken in the eggs, and then dredge in the panko-Parmesan mixture, coating thoroughly. Shake off any excess. Make sure the oil is hot by flicking a bit of flour or panko into the pan. If it sizzles, it's ready.

Add the chicken breasts and let cook without moving about 3 minutes, or until golden brown underneath. Carefully flip and continue cooking another 2 to 3 minutes, or until cooked through. Season with salt and pepper, garnish with flat-leaf parsley, spritz with fresh lemon, and enjoy with a crisp green salad. (If not serving immediately, remove the breasts from the pan while slightly undercooked and place on a wire rack in a 250-degree oven to keep warm until ready to eat.)

ingredients

- 2 boneless, skinless chicken breasts
- ¼ cup all-purpose flour
  Kosher salt and freshly ground black pepper to taste
- 2 large eggs
- ½ cup panko (Japanese breadcrumbs)
- ½ cup freshly grated Parmesan cheese
- ⅓ cup canola oil
- 2 tablespoons minced fresh flat-leaf parsley
  Lemon wedges for spritzing

variations

Mix in thyme and savory with the panko before breading. Achieve a pretty presentation by topping the chicken with the Arugula Salad with Lemon Vinaigrette (page 47).

halibut tacos with chipotle sour cream

The recipe for a perfect summer date: Take one recipe of Halibut Tacos, add one bucket of ice-cold beer, and stir in one very happy couple. What makes these fish tacos different is the earthy smokiness of the chipotle sauce, which is also delicious drizzled on grilled pork loin or flank steak.

prep time: 20 minutes | *cooking time:* 5 minutes | *yields:* 2 servings

For the Chipotle Sour Cream, combine the chipotle peppers, tomato, and garlic in a food processor. Pulse until smooth.

Place the sour cream in a small bowl and stir in 1 tablespoon of the chipotle mixture. Taste, continuing to add more of the chipotle mixture until the desired degree of spiciness is reached. Freeze the remaining chipotle mixture in an airtight container to use later in salsas, tortilla soup, or as a spicy condiment; it will last for months.

For the tacos, set a medium sauté pan over medium-high heat. Add the butter and canola oil. Season the halibut with salt and pepper. Dip the fish into the beaten egg and then dredge in the breadcrumbs, coating thoroughly. Fry the halibut until golden brown, about 2 minutes per side. Drain on paper towels and roll up with warm corn or flour tortillas and the Chipotle Sour Cream. Garnish with crunchy cabbage, a few leaves of cilantro, a spritz of fresh lime, and an ice-cold beer.

ingredients

chipotle sour cream

1   (7-ounce) can chipotles in adobo sauce

1   medium tomato, seeded and roughly chopped

4   cloves garlic

⅓ cup sour cream

fish tacos

2   tablespoons unsalted butter

3   tablespoons canola oil

7   ounces halibut, cut into 2-inch pieces

½ teaspoon kosher salt

¼ teaspoon freshly ground black pepper

1   egg, beaten

½ cup breadcrumbs

4   corn or flour tortillas

½ cup shredded napa or red cabbage for garnish

Fresh cilantro leaves for garnish

Lime wedges for garnish

variations

Instead of frying, grill the halibut in once piece and cut into 2-inch slices after it has cooked. Add diced tomatoes and sliced red or green onions.

pasta with cauliflower and pancetta

This is such a surprisingly delicious combination of ingredients. Its earthy flavors remind me of the ingredient-focused cuisine of the Pacific Northwest and the vibrant restaurant scene in my hometown of Portland. Don't be tempted to omit the horseradish. Trust me: the result is subtle and delicious, and the pecorino and cauliflower set it off perfectly.

ingredients

- 1 head cauliflower, cut into florets
- 4 tablespoons olive oil, divided
- Kosher salt and freshly ground black pepper
- 1 pound spaghetti
- 4 slices pancetta
- 4 leeks, white and light green parts only, thinly sliced
- 2 cloves garlic, minced
- 1½ cups heavy cream
- 2 teaspoons bottled horseradish
- ¼ cup grated pecorino cheese, plus more for garnish
- Freshly grated nutmeg to taste
- ¼ cup chopped fresh flat-leaf parsley

variations

Use grilled fennel or asparagus instead of the cauliflower, and add green peas. Prosciutto or bacon can replace the pancetta.

prep time: 15 minutes | *cooking time:* 50 minutes | *yields:* 4 servings

Preheat the oven to 375 degrees. Place the cauliflower on the baking sheet, drizzle with 2 tablespoons of the olive oil, and season with salt and pepper. Toss to coat evenly with the oil. Roast for 20 to 30 minutes, turning once or twice until tender inside and golden brown outside.

Bring a large pot of salted water to a boil and cook the spaghetti according to package directions until *al dente*. Reserve ½ cup of the cooking liquid. Drain and toss the pasta with the remaining 2 tablespoons of olive oil. Return to the cooking pan, and cover to keep warm.

While the cauliflower is roasting and the water is coming to a boil, set a large sauté pan over medium heat. Add the pancetta and cook until crispy, about 5 minutes. Drain on paper towels and crumble into bite-size pieces, reserving the rendered fat in the pan.

Add the leeks to the same pan and sauté until soft, about 4 or 5 minutes. Add the garlic and sauté for 2 minutes. Add the leeks and garlic to the reserved pasta while you continue preparing the sauce.

Add the cream, horseradish, and pecorino to the sauté pan and bring just to a boil. Remove from the heat and season with salt, pepper, and nutmeg to taste. Add the reserved pasta and leek mixture. Toss to combine. If the sauce seems too thick, return to the heat and add some of the reserved pasta water to the pan. Cook just until the desired consistency is reached.

Add the reserved pancetta, roasted cauliflower, and parsley. Toss to combine and serve immediately. Serve with extra pecorino.

spinach and mushroom lasagne

This dish will please vegetarians and meat-eaters alike. It's a little labor-intensive, but the result is very pretty and freezes well. Your work will not go unnoticed here. Just be sure to use freshly grated nutmeg, as it really brings out the flavors of the cheese and spinach. Look for whole nutmeg in the bulk spice aisle of your natural foods store.

ingredients

noodles

9 sheets lasagne noodles

sauce

1 tablespoon olive oil

1 small yellow onion, chopped

6 cloves garlic, minced

1 (28-ounce) can crushed tomatoes, with juice

1 tablespoon tomato paste

2 bay leaves

1 tablespoon red wine vinegar

1 teaspoon ground oregano

1 teaspoon kosher salt

1 teaspoon freshly ground black pepper

mushroom layer

1 tablespoon olive oil

3 cups thinly sliced button mushrooms

3 cups thinly sliced cremini mushrooms

Kosher salt and freshly ground black pepper to taste

spinach layer

2 (9-ounce) bags spinach, roughly chopped

1 teaspoon freshly grated nutmeg

1 teaspoon kosher salt

prep time: 40 minutes | *cooking time:* 90 minutes | *yields:* 6 servings

For best results in preparing the noodles, bring a large pot of salted water to a boil over high heat and cook the noodles according to package directions until *al dente*. Alternatively, use no-boil noodles: Fill a large pot with very hot tap water. Add all the noodles, one at a time to help prevent sticking, and let soak for 5 minutes. Remove from the water and place in a single layer on a clean kitchen towel. Or, use dry noodles and pour ½ cup of water over the last layer of sauce when assembling the dish.

To prepare the sauce, set a large saucepan over medium heat and add the oil. Sauté the onion for 2 or 3 minutes. Add the garlic and sauté 1 to 2 minutes. Add the crushed tomatoes, tomato paste, bay leaves, vinegar, oregano, salt, and pepper, stirring to combine. Bring to a simmer and let cook for 35 minutes.

While the sauce is simmering, prepare the other layers for the lasagne.

For the mushrooms, place a large, nonstick sauté pan over medium-high heat and add the oil. Add the mushrooms and sprinkle with salt and pepper. Toss to coat with the oil. Sauté 2 to 3 minutes, or until the mushrooms have released their moisture. Continue cooking until the mushrooms just start to brown, and then remove from the heat.

For the spinach, set a large saucepan over medium-high heat and add 1 tablespoon of water. Add the spinach, nutmeg, and salt. Cook until the spinach is just wilted, but still bright green. Place the spinach in a clean kitchen towel and squeeze to remove as much liquid as possible. Alternatively, place in a sieve and press the spinach with the back of a spoon to drain the water. *(continued)*

spinach and mushroom lasagne *(continued)*

ingredients

cottage-cheese layer

1 (16-ounce) container low-fat cottage cheese

¼ cup chopped fresh flat-leaf parsley

¼ cup freshly grated Parmesan cheese

2 teaspoons freshly grated nutmeg

1 teaspoon freshly ground black pepper

fresh cheeses

24 ounces fresh mozzarella, sliced

½ cup freshly grated Parmesan cheese

variations

Add a pound of cooked ground beef, pork, or veal to the sauce to please meat lovers. Try sautéed broccoli rabe instead of spinach. For an incredible level of decadence, pour a béchamel sauce over the top of the lasagna before baking.

prep time: 40 minutes | *cooking time:* 90 minutes | *yields:* 6 servings

For the cottage-cheese layer, combine the cottage cheese, parsley, Parmesan, nutmeg, and pepper in a small bowl.

Preheat the oven to 375 and assemble the lasagne:

1. Spread 3 tablespoons of the sauce in the bottom of a 13 x 9 x 2-inch casserole dish.

2. Add a single layer of noodles across the bottom of the dish, overlapping slightly to form the base of the lasagne.

3. Spread half of the cottage cheese mixture over the noodles.

4. Sprinkle half of the mushrooms over the cheese.

5. Distribute half of the spinach over the mushrooms.

6. Set half of the mozzarella slices evenly over the noodles.

7. Spoon in half of the remaining sauce and spread evenly.

8. Add another single layer of noodles.

9. Repeat the layers: cottage cheese, mushrooms, spinach, noodles, sauce, and mozzarella.

10. Top with the grated Parmesan.

Bake for 50 minutes, or until bubbly and golden brown. Remove from the oven and let rest for 10 minutes for the layers to set. Serve with the Arugula with Shaved Parmesan and Lemon Vinaigrette (page 47) for a bright contrast to the rich lasagne.

blue cheese mashed potatoes

I love blue cheese and the way its creamy, tangy flavor pairs perfectly with a rich, juicy steak.
The potatoes taste even better shared with the person I love most. After one bite, you'll want
to create more special occasions to warrant this meal. If you somehow have leftovers, you can
pat the cold mashed potatoes into little patties and fry them in a bit of butter for a delicious
potato cake the next night.

prep time: 10 minutes | *cooking time:* 15 minutes | *yields:* 2 servings

Bring a small pan of water to a boil. Add the potatoes and cook until soft. Drain the potatoes, reserving ½ cup of the potato water in a separate bowl.

While the potatoes are cooking, whip the crème fraîche and blue cheese together in a large bowl with a hand mixer until smooth. (Alternatively, you can whisk by hand, and use a potato masher for the potatoes.) Season with salt and pepper, and stir to combine. Add the cooked potatoes and beat until just smooth; be careful to not overbeat, as the potatoes can turn gluey. If the mixture seems too thick, drizzle in the reserved potato water until the desired consistency is reached. Season with more salt and pepper if needed, and garnish with chives.

ingredients

2   medium to large russet potatoes, peeled and cut into 2-inch pieces

½ cup crème fraîche

¼ cup crumbled blue cheese

Kosher salt and freshly ground black pepper to taste

Chopped fresh chives for garnish

variations

Beat in roasted garlic in lieu of blue cheese, or grated Romano for a milder cheese flavor.

pan-seared rib-eye for two

Good red meat is a real occasion food, so pull out all the stops. Rib-eye is one of the most flavorful cuts of steak, and if you can find USDA prime, you've got a good night ahead. Go for dry-aged, too, if you've got the budget; it's all the better but not required. Usually I pan-sear the steak, but you can also grill it with fabulous results. Serve it with my Blue Cheese Mashed Potatoes (page 89) and a crisp green salad.

prep time: 5 minutes | *cooking time:* 15 minutes | *yields:* 2 servings

Set a cast-iron or heavy skillet over high heat. Generously season the steak with salt and pepper. When the pan is very hot, add the steak and reduce the heat to medium-high. To create a nice sear, do not move the steak. Let it cook until nicely browned, about 4 minutes. Flip once and continue cooking another 4 to 5 minutes for medium-rare. Remove from the heat and let rest 5 minutes.

Alternatively, cook the steaks in a pre-heated, heavy, oven-safe pan under the broiler, or grill outside.

While the meat is resting, add the beef broth to the hot skillet and bring to a boil, scraping up any browned bits with a wooden spoon. Lower the heat and simmer until broth has reduced to ¼ cup. Remove the pan from the heat and add the butter, gently swirling in the pan to create a silky, shiny sauce.

Slice the rib-eye against the grain and drizzle with the pan sauce. Serve with generous scoop of Blue Cheese Mashed Potatoes (page 89).

ingredients

1 (12- to 16-ounce) rib-eye steak, Prime or Choice grade

   Kosher salt and freshly ground black pepper

¾ cup low-sodium beef broth

3 tablespoons unsalted butter, chilled

variations

Top rib-eye with crispy-fried onions for steak-house flavor.

roasted chicken with new potatoes

Roast chicken is the ultimate expression of love. It makes people feel that you're taking care of them—and that's a skill worth mastering! I recommend starting the chicken in a hot oven to crisp the skin first, and then turning the temperature down to roast slowly and keep the meat moist. When it's done, be patient and allow the chicken to rest for 15 minutes before carving. A chicken this size will serve four, but I like to make a big one even for two people. You can use the leftovers for Roasted Chicken Salad with Roasted Beets and Gorgonzola (page 43).

ingredients

prep time: 15 minutes | *cooking time:* 1 hour 20 minutes | *yields:* 4 servings

chicken

- 1 (6½-pound) roaster chicken
- 4 tablespoons (½ stick) unsalted butter, cubed
- 1 lemon, quartered
- 1 small yellow onion, quartered
- 1 teaspoon herbes de Provence
  Kosher salt and freshly ground black pepper to taste

new potatoes

- 1 pound new potatoes, scrubbed clean, patted dry, and cut in half
- 2 tablespoons olive oil
- ½ teaspoon kosher salt
- ¼ teaspoon freshly ground black pepper

variations

Try a variety of fresh herbs stuffed under the skin: rosemary, sage, parsley, and thyme. Add root vegetables to the roasting pan for an autumnal dinner.

Preheat the oven to 450 degrees. Rinse the chicken inside and out with cold water. Pat dry. Separate the skin from the breasts and massage about half the butter into the meat under the skin. Massage the remaining butter on the outside of the bird. Place the lemon and onion wedges into the cavity. Sprinkle the bird, inside and out, with the herbes de Provence and a generous seasoning of salt and pepper.

Set the chicken in a roasting pan and roast uncovered for 20 minutes. While the chicken is roasting, prepare the potatoes. Place the potatoes on a rimmed baking sheet, drizzle with the olive oil, and season with salt and pepper. Toss to distribute the oil and seasonings evenly.

After the first 20 minutes of roasting, reduce the oven to 325 and set a timer for 1 hour. After 30 minutes, add the potatoes to the oven. Roast the chicken and potatoes, turning the potatoes 3 to 4 times during the cooking time. Remove the chicken from the oven when the timer buzzes, and tent with aluminum foil to rest for 15 minutes. Leave the potatoes in the oven to finish cooking, if necessary, while the chicken rests. Carve the chicken, saving any juices to pour at the table. Serve with a fresh green salad for a completely delightful meal.

classic cook-off chili

This is our contribution to the Beverly Hills Chili Cook-Off every summer (we couldn't believe they had one either). Though we haven't won (yet), this version is completely divine. Go ahead and use 80-percent lean beef—the extra fat has a good payoff. Good luck in your own "cook-offs." Let me know if you win.

ingredients

- 2 tablespoons vegetable oil
- 1 medium-size yellow onion, diced
- 2 tablespoons chile powder
- 1 tablespoon ground cumin
- 1 teaspoon ground oregano
- 1 teaspoon cayenne pepper
- 1 pound ground beef
- 1 green bell pepper, finely chopped
- 5 cloves garlic, minced
- 1 jalapeño, seeded and minced
- 1 tablespoon tomato paste
- 1 (32-ounce) carton low-sodium chicken broth (4 cups)
- 1 (28-ounce) can diced plum tomatoes, with juice
- 1 (15-ounce) can pinto beans, rinsed and drained
- Kosher salt and freshly ground black pepper to taste
- Sour cream for garnish
- Cheddar cheese for garnish
- Chopped green onion for garnish

variations

Feel free to use ground turkey, chicken, Italian sausage, or a combination, and leave out the beans if you're from Texas.

prep time: 15 minutes | *cooking time:* 1½ hours | *yields:* 8 servings

Set a Dutch oven over medium-high heat and add the oil. Add the onion and sauté until translucent, about 3 minutes. Stir in the chile powder, cumin, oregano, and cayenne. Cook, stirring frequently, for 1 minute. Add the ground beef, breaking up the meat as it cooks. Add the bell pepper, garlic, and jalapeño, and cook until soft.

Drain the excess grease from the meat. Add the tomato paste and chicken broth, and bring to a boil. Reduce the heat, cover, and simmer for 30 minutes. Add the tomatoes (with their juice) and the beans. Season with salt and pepper. Simmer another 30 minutes to an hour. Serve with sour cream, Cheddar cheese, and green onion on the side.

lake como-style salmon

One summer Fritz and I traveled to Italy, where we spent a month painting the landscape and eating wonderfully fresh local ingredients around Lake Como. On a visit to L'Isola Comacina, a tiny little island in the lake, we had the most wonderful fish. They prepared it in parchment and then drenched it in fresh lemon juice and first-press olive oil. For a tableside flourish, they shaved an obscene amount of salt from a brick of salt onto the fish. To our pleasant surprise, the fish did not taste salty. It merely tasted flavorful. The simplicity of this dish depends on the highest-quality ingredients, so use the freshest you can find and the best you can afford.

prep time: 5 minutes | *cooking time:* 10 minutes | *yields:* 4 servings

Place a baking sheet in the oven and preheat to 475 degrees. Tear a large piece of parchment and aluminum foil, and set the parchment on the foil. Place the salmon, skin-side down, on the parchment. Sprinkle with the oregano leaves, drizzle with 1 tablespooon of the lemon juice, and season lightly with salt.

Wrap the parchment and foil together, crimping the edges well, but leaving a bit of room for steam in the packet. Set the packet on the preheated baking sheet and bake until the packet puffs up with steam and the salmon is barely cooked through, 8 to 10 minutes.

Remove the salmon from the foil, being careful of any hot steam, and place on a serving platter. Drizzle with the remaining lemon juice and the olive oil. Sprinkle with more salt and season with pepper. Garnish with the snipped chives. Let stand for several minutes for the lemon and olive oil to permeate the fish. Serve warm or at room temperature.

ingredients

1¼ pounds salmon fillet, skin-on

2 sprigs oregano, stems discarded

⅓ cup freshly squeezed lemon juice (about 2 medium lemons), divided

Sea salt to taste

2 tablespoons extra-virgin olive oil

Freshly ground black pepper to taste

1 teaspoon snipped fresh chives

variations

Try this with rainbow trout, striped bass, or other lake fish.

veal stew with hungarian paprika

Stews always taste better on the second day, so you might want to make this on a Sunday afternoon in anticipation of a hectic work week. We always buy fresh peppers and roast them ourselves over the gas flame of the stovetop, but you can use jarred roasted red peppers if you wish. This stew begs to be served alongside buttered egg noodles and hearty brown bread, with a small crisp salad.

ingredients

- 3 tablespoons olive oil, divided
- 1¼ pounds boneless veal shoulder, cut into 1-inch pieces
- 1 small onion, thinly sliced
- 1 clove garlic, minced
- 1 tablespoon all-purpose flour
- 1 tablespoon sweet Hungarian paprika
- 2 cups low-sodium chicken broth
- 2 teaspoons tomato paste
- 1 red bell pepper
- 8 ounces button mushrooms, cut in half
- ½ teaspoon kosher salt
- ½ teaspoon freshly ground black pepper
- Sour cream for garnish
- Fresh dill for garnish

variations

Substitute pork shoulder or chicken thighs for the veal for a more economical meal.

prep time: 20 minutes | *cooking time:* 1½ hours | *yields:* 4 servings

Set a Dutch oven over medium heat and add 2 tablespoons of the oil. Add the veal and brown on all sides. (Take your time with this process. Browning the meat will create *fond*, the browned bits that stick to the bottom of the pan and give the stew such depth of flavor.) Remove the browned veal and set aside.

Reduce the heat to medium-low and add the onion. Cook until soft, about 5 minutes. Add the garlic and cook 2 minutes more. Add the flour and paprika and cook another minute to remove any raw flour taste, stirring constantly. Stir in the chicken broth and tomato paste, and bring to a boil over high heat. Return the veal to the Dutch oven, reduce the heat, and cover. Simmer for 1 hour, or until the veal is very tender.

While the stew is simmering, preheat the oven to 450 degrees. Place the bell pepper directly on a rack in the oven with a sheet pan placed on the rack below to catch any juices. Roast for 15 minutes, or until the skin darkens and begins to char. Alternatively, set the bell pepper directly above the flame on a gas stovetop. Turn with metal tongs until each side is blackened. Place the charred pepper in a plastic or paper bag, seal, and let steam for 5 minutes. When the pepper is cool enough to handle, rub away the blackened skin with your hands—it's okay if a few bits remain. Discard the seeds, core, and membrane from the pepper, and dice the roasted flesh.

Set a large skillet over medium-high heat and add the remaining tablespoon of olive oil. Add the mushrooms and season with salt and pepper. Sauté, stirring often, until the mushrooms have released their liquid and are beginning to brown. Add the sautéed mushrooms and the roasted pepper to the goulash. Simmer 10 more minutes to let the flavors meld. Garnish with a dollop of sour cream and sprinkling of fresh dill. Serve over buttered egg noodles or with dark pumpernickel for dipping.

garlic-thyme rack of lamb

Rack of lamb is a seriously impressive dinner. Like meet-the-parents impressive. So save this dinner for an occasion when you really want to impress. A "frenched" rack of lamb has the fat and strands of meat trimmed from the long ends of the bones, which makes for an elegant presentation. Ask your butcher to french the lamb for you. Want to really wow your guests? Cut the rack in half and stand both halves on end, intertwining the bones, and set upright on a plate on top of the Mint Chimichurri (page 102).

prep time: 5 minutes	*cooking time:* 30 minutes	*yields:* 4 servings

Preheat the oven to 350 degrees. Set a large, heavy skillet over high heat and add 1 tablespoon of the olive oil. Pat the lamb completely dry and season generously with salt and pepper, rubbing the seasoning into the meat for maximum taste. Brown the lamb well on all sides, about 8 minutes.

Place the garlic, parsley, thyme, and remaining 3 tablespoons of olive oil in the bowl of a food processor and blend to a coarse paste. Coat the browned lamb with the herb mixture and place in a shallow baking dish. Roast in the oven for 15 to 20 minutes, or until an instant-read thermometer inserted into the center of the meat registers 120 degrees for medium-rare.

Remove the lamb from heat and cover loosely with aluminum foil. Let rest 10 minutes. The lamb will continue cooking, rising 5 to 10 degrees during this time, and the juices will redistribute throughout the meat. Slice each rack into individual chops and serve hot with the Mint Chimichurri (page 102).

ingredients

- 4 tablespoons olive oil, divided
- 1 (8-rib) rack of lamb, frenched
- 2 teaspoons kosher salt
- 2 teaspoons coarsely ground black pepper
- 4 large cloves garlic
- ⅓ cup fresh flat-leaf parsley leaves
- 1 tablespoon fresh thyme or 1 teaspoon dried thyme
- Mint Chimichurri (page 102)

variations

Use crown roast of pork and roast until an instant-read thermometer registers 150 degrees. Add chopped fresh rosemary to the rub. Place fluted paper frills on the bones for added festivity.

mint chimichurri

This popular Argentine sauce is traditionally served on beef, but it works on all kinds of meats. Here I've added mint, which makes it a wonderful companion to the Garlic-Thyme Rack of Lamb (page 101).

ingredients

- 3 tablespoons red wine vinegar
- 2 tablespoons water
- ¾ teaspoon kosher salt
- ¼ cup extra-virgin olive oil
- 4 cloves garlic, minced
- ½ bay leaf
- ½ teaspoon red pepper flakes
- ½ teaspoon freshly ground black pepper
- ¼ cup finely chopped fresh flat-leaf parsley
- ⅓ cup finely chopped fresh mint

variations

For a zippy topping to the Grilled Flank Steak (page 107), replace the mint with cilantro and the vinegar with lime juice. To show off your culinary muscle and coax even more flavor from the herbs, use a mortar and pestle instead of chopping by hand. Use roasted garlic instead of fresh for a milder taste.

prep time: 10 minutes | *melding time:* 30 minutes | *yields:* ¾ cup

Stir together the vinegar, water, and salt in a medium bowl until the salt dissolves. Whisk in the oil. Stir in the garlic, bay leaf, red pepper flakes, black pepper, parsley, and mint.

Let stand for 30 minutes at room temperature for the flavors to meld. Discard the bay leaf and stir before serving.

jerk pork loin with habanero salsa

Caribbean food tastes slow-cooked, but this one won't keep you in the kitchen all day. This dish has all the flavors of a great date: it's sweet, spicy, and hot, and it keeps you coming back for more. Fritz loves to slice and dice and chop, so he makes the salsa while I put together the meat. The only trick is to chop the habanero very finely so that the flavor permeates the salsa. Don't worry if it's too hot at first; the heat will dissipate a little as the salsa rests. Remember to wear rubber or latex gloves when working with hot chiles like this; otherwise, you may have fiery fingertips for several days.

prep time: 15 minutes | *cooking & marinating:* 1 hour | *yields:* 4 servings

To make the pork, combine the oil and all the spices. Rub all over the tenderloin, massaging the spices into the meat. Place in a large, resealable plastic bag and refrigerate for 20 to 30 minutes to marinate.

While the pork is marinating, prepare the salsa. Combine all the ingredients in a small bowl. Cover and refrigerate until ready to serve.

Preheat the oven to 425 degrees. Place the tenderloin in a baking dish or small roasting pan and cook for 5 minutes. Lower the oven temperature to 325 degrees and continue roasting about 25 more minutes, or until an instant-read thermometer registers 140 to 145 degrees. Remove the pork from the oven and let rest for 5 minutes to allow the juices to redistribute. (After resting, the internal temperature should register 150 degrees; the interior should be juicy and may be slightly pink.) Slice, and spoon with the salsa. Serve with Coconut Black Beans (page 106) and steamed white rice.

ingredients

pork

- 1 tablespoon canola oil
- ½ teaspoon ground cinnamon
- ½ teaspoon freshly grated nutmeg
- ½ teaspoon allspice
- ½ teaspoon dried oregano
- ½ teaspoon kosher salt
- ½ teaspoon freshly ground black pepper
- 1½ pounds pork tenderloin

salsa

- 1 ripe mango, diced
- ½ cup red onion, diced
- Juice of 1 medium lime
- ⅓ cup chopped fresh cilantro
- 1 small tomato, seeded and diced
- ½ habanero pepper, minced
- 1 clove garlic, minced
- 1 tablespoon olive oil

variations

Grill the pork instead of roasting, and serve the slices wrapped in corn or flour tortillas with sour cream. Substitute pineapple for mango.

coconut black beans

The creamy coconut milk in this dish cools down a spicy main course like the Jerk Pork Loin with Habanero Salsa (page 105). For a complete meal for your vegetarian sweetheart, serve these beans with rice, avocado, and sautéed plantains.

ingredients

prep time: 5 minutes | *cooking time:* 25 minutes | *yields:* 4 servings

- 1 teaspoon vegetable oil
- 1 clove garlic, minced
- 1 shallot, minced
- 1 (30-ounce) can black beans, rinsed and drained
- 1 (14-ounce) can coconut milk
  Tabasco sauce to taste
  Kosher salt to taste

variations

Add a minced mango to make it even sweeter. Transform the dish into a Thai dessert by holding off on the spices and sweetening with sugar. Serve chilled with sticky rice.

Set a medium saucepan over medium heat and add the vegetable oil. Sauté the garlic and shallot until soft but not browned, about 3 minutes. Add the black beans and coconut milk. Season with Tabasco and salt to taste. Simmer 15 to 20 minutes, or until the coconut milk is slightly reduced and thickened. Check the seasonings again, adding more if necessary, and serve hot.

grilled flank steak

The key to making a great flank steak is to not overcook it. Cooked medium-rare and sliced on the bias, this rather tough cut of meat is fabulous. Cooked medium-well, it turns to shoe leather. The meat comes to life with a bit of chimichurri. We have a recipe for Mint Chimichurri on page 102. For flank steak, replace the mint with cilantro or parsley and the vinegar with lime or lemon juice.

prep and cooking: 20 minutes | *marinating:* 1-3 hours | *yields:* 6 servings

In a glass baking dish large enough to hold the flank steak, whisk together the oil, red wine vinegar, garlic, onion powder, salt, and sugar. Place the steak in the baking dish and refrigerate, turning every 30 minutes for 1 to 3 hours.

Prepare a medium-hot grill and cook the flank steak for 5 minutes. Turn once and continue cooking for 2 to 3 minutes for medium-rare or 3 to 5 minutes for medium. Remove from the grill and let rest on a carving board for 5 to 10 minutes to let the juices redistribute. To serve, slice thinly against the grain on the bias.

ingredients

½ cup canola oil

1 cup red wine vinegar

1 teaspoon chopped fresh garlic

½ teaspoon onion powder

1 teaspoon kosher salt

1 teaspoon sugar

1 pound flank steak

variations

Try this on grilled pita with chopped cucumbers, oregano, and yogurt. This can also be served with Blue Cheese Mashed Potatoes (page 89) and Green Garden Salad (page 46). The leftovers are perfect for lunch on a toasted buttered baguette.

herb-roasted cornish hens

Usher in autumn with this lovely dish. Cornish hens make a nice presentation—everyone gets his or own little bird—and I think they have better flavor than chicken, especially when roasted with bay leaves, fresh sage, and thyme. Don't bother fumbling around with a knife and fork for too long. At some point you just have to use your hands!

ingredients

prep time: 5 minutes | *cooking time:* 50 minutes | *yields:* 2 servings

- 2 tablespoons freshly squeezed lemon juice (1 small lemon)
- 2 garlic cloves, minced
  Kosher salt and freshly ground black pepper to taste
- 2 bay leaves
- 2 sprigs sage
- 2 sprigs thyme
- 1 tablespoon olive oil
- 2 Cornish game hens (1½ pounds each), giblets removed
- ¾ cup low-sodium chicken broth
- ½ tablespoon honey
- 1½ tablespoons unsalted butter, chilled

variations

Create a savory-sweet combination by coating the birds with red currant jelly and a sprinkling of fresh rosemary. Replace the honey with the jelly for the sauce.

Preheat the oven to 425 degrees. Rinse the hens with cold water and pat dry. Sprinkle the cavity of each hen with a tablespoon of lemon juice and rub with minced garlic. Season generously with salt and pepper, inside and out. Place a bay leaf and a sprig of sage and thyme into each hen. Tie the legs together with kitchen twine for even cooking and tuck the wing tips under the hen for a more attractive presentation.

Place the hens on roasting rack in large baking dish or roasting pan. Drizzle the hens with olive oil and massage into the skin. Season with additional salt and pepper if needed. Roast until hens are cooked through and an instant-read thermometer registers 170 to 175 degrees, or until the juices run clear when thickest part of thigh is pierced, about 40 minutes.

Pour the juices and any browned bits from the roasting pan into a sauté pan. Add the chicken broth and bring to a boil over high heat. Lower the heat and simmer 5 minutes to thicken slightly. Add the honey and simmer another minute. Remove from heat and swirl in the cold butter. Serve the hens with the sauce, a garden salad, and fresh bread.

lamb vindaloo

Stewed lamb and Indian spices are a combination like no other. You can find a vindaloo spice mix or paste at Indian food stores if you lack a cupboard of spices at home. This recipe isn't as spicy as traditional vindaloo—it only calls for 1/8 teaspoon of cayenne—but you could add some of your favorite dried red chiles to the mixture and see just how hot you can take it.

prep time: 15 minutes | *cooking time:* 55 minutes | *yields:* 4 servings

Place the vinegar, garlic, curry powder, cumin, ginger, cardamom, cinnamon, cloves, cayenne, mustard seed, and 2 tablespoons of the olive oil in the bowl of a food processor. Blend until smooth. Place the spice mixture in a large bowl. Add the lamb and toss to coat thoroughly.

Set a large, heavy saucepan over medium-high heat and add the remaining 2 tablespoons of olive oil. Add the onions and sauté 5 minutes, or until softened and golden. Add the lamb and cook 5 minutes more to brown. Add the tomatoes, scraping up any browned bits from the bottom of the pan. Bring to a boil, reduce the heat, and cover. Gently simmer 45 minutes, or until the lamb is tender, stirring occasionally.

Season to taste with salt and pepper. Stir in the cilantro and serve hot with steamed rice and naan or grilled pita bread. Top with yogurt to cut the spiciness if needed.

ingredients

1/3 cup apple cider vinegar

4 large cloves garlic

2 teaspoons curry powder

2 teaspoons ground cumin

1 teaspoon ground ginger

3/4 teaspoon ground cardamom

1/2 teaspoon ground cinnamon

1/4 teaspoon ground cloves

1/8 teaspoon cayenne pepper, or more to taste

1 tablespoon yellow mustard seeds or 2 teaspoons Dijon mustard

4 tablespoons olive oil, divided

1 1/4 pounds lamb stew meat, cut into 2-inch pieces

1 medium onion, chopped

1 (14 1/2-ounce) can crushed tomatoes, with juice

Kosher salt and freshly ground black pepper to taste

1/2 cup chopped cilantro

Plain yogurt for garnish (optional)

variations

Instead of making into a stew, skewer the spiced lamb with chopped bell pepper and grill or broil. You can also substitute roasted vegetables for the lamb.

pappardelle bolognese

The chopping and stirring are fun to do together; start the date night when you turn on the stove, not when you sit down to eat. You can make pasta sauces as spicy, sweet, or savory as you want them to be. Experiment with different proportions. No matter how you do it, you'll find this a hearty and comforting meal that's also easy to prepare. Make it the night before for a truly stress-free date night. The sauce will only improve.

ingredients

prep time: 15 minutes | *cooking time:* 1½ hours | *yields:* 4 servings

- 2 tablespoons olive oil
- 1 medium onion, finely chopped
- 2 stalks celery, finely chopped
- 3 cloves garlic, minced
- ½ pound ground veal
- ½ pound ground pork
- 4 ounces pancetta, finely chopped
- 1 (14½-ounce) can crushed tomatoes, with juice
- 1 cup low-sodium chicken broth, plus more for thinning sauce
- ½ cup whole milk
- 2 sprigs thyme
- ¼ teaspoon kosher salt
- ⅛ teaspoon freshly ground black pepper
- 1 pound pappardelle or fettuccine
-    Freshly grated Parmesan cheese for garnish

variations

Replace the ground pork and veal with a combination of hot and sweet Italian sausage. Add sliced and sautéed mushrooms.

Set a large, heavy pot over medium heat and add the oil. Add the onions, celery, and garlic and sauté for 10 minutes, or until the vegetables soften and begin to brown. Increase the heat to high and add ground veal, ground pork, and pancetta. Cook for 10 minutes, or until the meat is browned, stirring frequently to break the meat into small pieces.

Drain off any excess grease, and stir in the tomatoes, chicken broth, milk, thyme, salt, and pepper. Reduce the heat to medium-low and simmer for 1 hour, stirring occasionally. Add more broth if the sauce gets too thick. Remove the thyme sprigs. Taste and season with more salt and pepper if needed. The sauce can be stored in an airtight container and refrigerated 2 days in advance or frozen up to 2 weeks in advance.

To prepare the pasta, bring a large pot of salted water to a boil and cook the pappardelle according to package directions until *al dente*. Drain and toss with the bolognese sauce to combine. Garnish with fresh Parmesan and serve immediately.

bourbon-smothered pork chops

Anything smothered is a staple in the world of comfort food, and the addition of bourbon or whisky—we like Southern Comfort®—imparts a mysterious flavor to this down-home recipe. For maximum effect, serve with a generous scoop of mashed potatoes and sautéed green beans. You can use any bourbon or whisky you like, but serve up a little comfort after dinner to savor the throaty warmth of this aptly named elixir.

prep time: 10 minutes | *cooking time:* 45 minutes | *yields:* 4 servings

Preheat the oven to 200 degrees. Combine the garlic salt, pepper, paprika, thyme, sage, and cayenne in a small bowl. Place ⅓ cup of the flour on a plate. Pat the pork chops completely dry with paper towels. Massage the pork chops with the spice mixture, and then dredge in the flour, shaking to remove any excess.

Set a large, heavy skillet over medium-high heat and pour enough oil to come ¼ inch up the sides. When the oil reaches 350 degrees or shimmers from a pinch of flour, add the pork chops and fry 2 to 3 minutes per side, or until golden brown and almost cooked through. Place on a plate and cover loosely with aluminum foil. Set in the oven to keep warm.

Pour off all but 2 tablespoons of the oil and return the skillet to medium heat. Add the onions to the skillet and cook for 5 minutes, scraping the bottom of the pan to release any browned bits. Add the apples and cook for 10 minutes more. Stir the remaining 2 tablespoons of flour into the onion mixture and cook, stirring constantly, until the flour turns golden brown, about 4 minutes. Whisk in the broth and bourbon, whisking constantly until the gravy is smooth and free of lumps. Increase the heat to medium-high and bring to a boil. Reduce the heat to medium-low and simmer for 10 to 12 minutes, or until the gravy has thickened to the desired consistency. Serve two pork chops per person, spoon with the hot gravy, and season with a twist or two of black pepper.

ingredients

- 1½ teaspoons garlic salt
- ½ teaspoon freshly ground black pepper
- 1 teaspoon sweet Hungarian paprika
- ¼ teaspoon dried thyme
- ¼ teaspoon dried sage
- ⅛ teaspoon cayenne pepper
- ⅓ cup plus 2 tablespoons all-purpose flour, divided
- 8 thin-cut pork cutlets (about 3 ounces each)
- Canola or vegetable oil for frying
- 1 small onion, cut in half and thinly sliced
- 2 medium-size green apples, peeled, cored, and thinly sliced
- 1¾ cups low-sodium beef broth
- 3 tablespoons Southern Comfort® or other bourbon or whisky

variations

For a German vibe, forgo the whisky for apple cider and add sauerkraut.

citrus pan-roasted halibut

Fritz and I often drive down to the Santa Monica Seafood Company to pick out fresh fish for dinner. When the halibut looks particularly good, we'll pan-roast it with butter, garlic, herbs, and citrus for a wonderfully spunky summer fish entrée. Serve the halibut with roasted peppers and zucchini: Cut the vegetables into 1- to 2-inch pieces, drizzle with olive oil, sprinkle with salt and pepper, and place in a 375 degree oven for 30 minutes, or until nicely roasted.

prep time: 10 minutes | *cooking time:* 15 minutes | *yields:* 4 servings

Preheat the oven to 375 degrees. Combine the butter, chervil, garlic, pepper, lemon zest, and orange zest in small bowl.

Set an ovenproof sauté pan over medium-high heat and add the oil. Pat the halibut completely dry with paper towels and season both sides with salt and pepper. Place the halibut pretty-side down in the sauté pan and cook for 4 minutes without disturbing, or until golden brown. Carefully turn the halibut over. Place the sauté pan in the oven for 6 to 8 minutes, or until the halibut is just shy of cooked through.

Place the fillets on serving plates and cover to keep warm.

Return the sauté pan to the stovetop over low heat and add the butter mixture. Stir, scraping up any browned bits, until the butter has melted and the zest is fragrant. Pour the butter sauce over halibut and serve immediately.

ingredients

- 4 tablespoons (½ stick) unsalted butter, room temperature
- 1 tablespoon chopped fresh chervil
- 1 clove garlic, minced
- ¼ teaspoon freshly ground black pepper, plus more to taste
- ½ teaspoon freshly grated lemon zest
- ½ teaspoon freshly grated orange zest
- 1 tablespoon olive oil
- 4 (1-inch-thick) halibut fillets (5 to 7 ounces each)
- Kosher salt to taste

variations

Try also red snapper, mahi-mahi, or prawns. You can substitute marjoram, summer savory, or flat-leaf parsley for the chervil.

spaghetti with sausage meatballs

Some men I know, when left to their own devices, will craft meatballs the size of grapefruit. On date night, you two can make meatballs together—of a size that will fit on a fork. Smaller meatballs absorb sauce better and cook more quickly. Make your own fresh breadcrumbs: Remove the crust from several slices of stale bread, break the bread into pieces, and pulse in a food processor until fine.

ingredients

prep time: 20 minutes | *cooking time:* 45 minutes | *yields:* 4 servings

meatballs

- 8 ounces ground turkey
- 8 ounces hot or sweet Italian turkey sausage, casings removed
- 1½ cups fresh breadcrumbs or Japanese panko
- ¼ cup freshly grated Parmesan cheese, plus more for garnish
- 2 tablespoons finely chopped fresh flat-leaf parsley
- 2 cloves garlic, minced
- 2 teaspoons fresh thyme or ½ teaspoon dried
- ¼ teaspoon kosher salt
- ⅛ teaspoon freshly ground black pepper

sauce

- 2 teaspoons olive oil
- 1 small onion, finely chopped
- 4 cloves garlic, minced
- 2 tablespoons finely chopped fresh flat-leaf parsley
- 1 (28-ounce) can crushed tomatoes, with juice
- ¼ teaspoon kosher salt
- ⅛ teaspoon freshly ground black pepper
- 1 pound spaghetti
  Freshly grated Parmesan for garnish

variations

Try using ground pork and veal instead of turkey.

Preheat the oven to 400 degrees. Line a baking sheet with aluminum foil and spray with nonstick cooking spray.

To make the meatballs, combine the ground turkey, sausage, breadcrumbs, Parmesan, parsley, garlic, thyme, salt, and pepper in a medium bowl. Do not overmix, as the meat may become tough. Form the mixture into 1-inch balls and place on the prepared baking sheet. Bake for 10 minutes, or until firm. They do not have to be cooked all the way through, as they will be cooked more in the sauce.

While the meatballs are baking, prepare the sauce. Add the oil to a large, nonstick skillet and set over medium heat. Add the onion and cook for 5 minutes, or until soft. Add the garlic and cook for 1 minute. Add the parsley and tomatoes, increase the heat, and bring to a boil. Reduce the heat and simmer for 12 minutes, or until the sauce thickens and reduces slightly. Taste and season with salt and pepper. Reduce the heat to low and add the meatballs to the sauce. Cover and simmer 10 more minutes, or until the meatballs are completely cooked through.

While the sauce is simmering, bring a large pot of salted water to a boil. Add the pasta and cook according to package directions until *al dente*. Drain the pasta and return to the pot. Toss the pasta with a cup of the sauce. Serve the pasta on dinner plates or in shallow bowls. Spoon with the sauce and top with the meatballs. Sprinkle with freshly grated Parmesan and serve immediately.

bouillabaisse

I've tried many different versions of this Provençal stew from many different menus, and all have exceptionally fresh seafood in common. For a very special pot, make your own fish or vegetable stock— well worth the labor—and use in place of the chicken. Traditional French presentation would call for a topping of aïoli, a homemade garlicky mayonnaise, or rouille, a purée of olive oil, chile peppers, garlic, and breadcrumbs. On weeknights, I whip up a quick-and-easy aïoli using store-bought mayonnaise.

prep time: 30 minutes	*cooking time:* 35 minutes	*yields:* 4 servings

Set a Dutch oven over medium-high heat and add the oil. Add the onion and fennel slices, and season with salt. Sauté until tender, about 8 minutes. Add a little more than half the minced garlic and sauté until fragrant. Add the tomatoes, parsley, bay leaves, thyme, chicken broth, and wine. Bring to a boil, reduce the heat, and simmer for 20 minutes.

While the soup is simmering, prepare the *aïoli*. Sprinkle the remaining minced garlic with a with a generous pinch of salt. Chop and mash the garlic, scraping it with the side of your knife blade into a paste. Combine the garlic paste with the mayonnaise, lemon juice, and cayenne. Cover with plastic wrap and refrigerate until ready to serve.

Season the broth with salt to taste. Add the snapper and halibut, cover, and cook for 2 minutes. Add the shrimp and clams, cover, and cook for 2 more minutes, or until the shrimp just turns pink.

Discard any unopened clams. Distribute the seafood and broth evenly among bowls. Garnish with the reserved fennel fronds. Serve immediately with crusty bread and a thick smear of *aïoli*.

ingredients

2	tablespoons olive oil
1	small white onion, sliced
1	fennel bulb, sliced, fronds reserved
	Kosher salt to taste
7	cloves garlic, minced, divided
1	(28-ounce) can whole plum tomatoes, with juice
6	sprigs flat-leaf parsley
2	bay leaves
½	teaspoon fresh thyme
3	cups low-sodium chicken broth
¾	cup dry white wine
½	pound snapper fillet, cut into 2-inch strips
½	pound halibut fillet, cut into 2-inch strips
8	medium (31- to 35-count) shrimp, tails on, shelled and deveined
8	small clams, cleaned
3	cloves garlic
1	cup mayonnaise
1½	tablespoons freshly squeezed lemon juice (½ medium lemon)
½	teaspoon cayenne pepper, or more to taste
	Toasted French bread for garnish

variations

Add or omit any seafood—the firmer the fish, the better. Stir in 2 tablespoons of Pernod just before serving for a real taste of Marseille.

french dip sandwich

A well-marbled rib roast, cooked until crispy and brown outside and perfectly pink inside, makes the perfect hot sandwiches, bathed liberally in beefy jus. Serve it with my French Potato Salad (page 49) or Cayenne Onion Rings (page 33) for a hearty and satisfying lunch or dinner. It's an easy, laid-back meal you'll enjoy cooking together—and one the man of the house may reprise for his buddies on poker night, too.

prep time: 10 minutes | *cooking time:* 1 hour 15 minutes | *yields:* 4 servings

Preheat the oven to 350 degrees. Rub the roast with the oil and sprinkle liberally with salt and pepper. Place in a shallow baking dish, and roast for 50 to 60 minutes, or until the meat registers 145 degrees on an instant-read thermometer for medium. (The temperature will continue to rise as the meat rests.) Remove the roast from the pan and transfer to a plate. Cover with foil and let rest 15 minutes for the juices to redistribute.

Turn off the oven and add the sandwich rolls to warm gently while the roast rests and you prepare the dipping jus.

Pour the beef broth into the baking dish and stir up any browned bits stuck to the bottom. Pour the broth and bits into a small saucepan and bring to a boil over high heat. Lower the heat to medium-high, and simmer until the broth has reduced by half, about 15 minutes. Remove from the heat and add the cold butter, swirling the pan until combined. Season with salt and pepper to taste, and pour into individual serving bowls.

Slice the meat thinly across the grain. Stuff each warmed roll with a generous portion of roast beef and serve au jus.

ingredients

- 2 pounds boneless rib roast
- 1 tablespoon olive oil
   Kosher salt and freshly ground black pepper
- 2 cups low-sodium beef broth
- 1 tablespoon unsalted butter, chilled
- 4 sandwich rolls, split in half lengthwise

variations

Purchase thinly sliced, rare roast beef from a deli for a quick-and-easy version. Make a spread of mayonnaise mixed with prepared horseradish. Slice and roast onions and peppers in a foil packet with the beef as a sandwich topping. Melt slices of Provolone in the sandwich rolls.

crispy tofu stir-fry with baby bok choy

Fresh baby bok choy, wild earthy mushrooms, and crispy-fried tofu combine for a marriage made in vegetarian heaven. You won't even notice the absence of meat in this dish—the meaty texture of firm tofu provides a believable (and yummy!) stand-in. But if one of you is a committed omnivore, you can always substitute sliced chicken breast for the tofu.

prep time: 15 minutes | *cooking time:* 10 minutes | *yields:* 4 servings

Prepare all the ingredients for stir-frying. Heat the oil in a wok or large, heavy skillet over medium-high heat until almost smoking.

Place the egg yolk in a shallow bowl and beat. Dip the tofu in the egg yolk to coat, and then roll in the breadcrumbs. Gently place the tofu in the hot oil and cook about 3 minutes, turning occasionally until golden brown. Transfer the tofu to a paper towel to drain.

Add the mushrooms and cook for about 3 minutes, stirring frequently, until lightly browned. Lower the heat to medium, and add the ginger, garlic, bok choy, and water. Cook for 4 minutes, stirring frequently. Add the green onions and oyster sauce, tossing to coat all the ingredients with the sauce. Place the bok choy on a serving platter and top with the crispy tofu. Serve with udon noodles or steamed rice.

ingredients

6 ounces firm tofu, cut into 1-inch squares, ½-inch thick

1 egg yolk

⅓ cup peanut oil

⅓ cup panko breadcrumbs

¾ pound mushrooms such as shitake, oyster, cremini, or a combination, sliced

1 tablespoon freshly grated ginger

3 cloves garlic, minced

1 pound baby bok choy, sliced thinly on the diagonal

1 tablespoon water

4 green onions, sliced thinly on the diagonal

3 tablespoons oyster sauce

variations

Substitute spinach, amaranth, or napa cabbage for the bok choy. Add sliced carrots or red bell pepper for extra crunch and color.

chapter five desserts

Here comes the sweet reward! Nothing says I love you like…well… pick any of the desserts in this chapter. They're all oozing with love, every single one, from old-fashioned Lemon Bars to silky Crème Brûlée and from rich Chocolate Ganache Cake to decidedly grown-up Coconut-Almond Candy Bars. After all of the hard work you've done putting the meal together, this is your time to relax, reflect, and reward yourselves. All you have to do now is eat cake and remember how lucky you are, how much you love your life and your Sweetie Pie.

coconut-almond candy bars

My good friends own a restaurant called ROUX in my hometown of Portland. On one of our visit, their pastry chef, Melissa, presented us with her deceivingly rich, handcrafted rendition of an Almond Joy. Here's a similar version you can make easily at home. Melissa serves hers with coconut ice cream, but these morsels are amply yummy on their own. I highly encourage you to use the best dark chocolate you can find for this.

ingredients

24 ounces high-quality dark chocolate, preferably at least 60-percent cacao, finely chopped, or 4 cups bittersweet chocolate morsels

1 pound confectioners' sugar

1 pound sweetened shredded coconut

3 tablespoons rum (optional)

1 (14-ounce) can sweetened condensed milk

8 tablespoons (1 stick) unsalted butter, room temperature

32 whole almonds, toasted

variations

While the final chocolate layer is still wet, sprinkle with toasted coconut or toasted chopped almonds. Make in miniature foil cupcake liners for circular treats.

prep time: 35 minutes | *setting time:* overnight | *yields:* 8 bars or 32 candies

Line a glass 13 x 9 x 2-inch baking dish with wax paper. Place 1½ cups of the chocolate in a microwave-safe glass container. Microwave on high at 20-second intervals, stirring between each interval until the chocolate is melted and completely smooth. Pour the chocolate onto the bottom of the prepared baking dish and spread evenly. Set aside to cool.

Using the paddle attachment of a stand mixer, mix the sugar, coconut, rum (if using), and condensed milk until well combined. Add the butter and beat well. Spread the coconut mixture evenly on top of the hardened chocolate. Cover with plastic wrap and chill overnight.

Remove the hardened chocolate-coconut layer from the pan, peeling off the wax paper from the bottom of the chocolate. For 6½-inch candy bars, cut the layer lengthwise into 4 strips and horizontally in half. Place 8 almonds neatly down the center of each strip.

For individual candies, cut the layer lengthwise into 4 strips and horizontally into 8 strips to form 32 squares. Press an almond in the top of each piece.

Place the remaining 2½ cups chocolate in a microwave-safe glass container. Microwave on high at 20-second intervals, stirring between each interval until the chocolate is melted and completely smooth.

Place a wire rack over wax paper. Set the chocolate-coconut-almond bars or squares on the rack and pour with the melted chocolate. Allow the chocolate to set, and then store in an airtight container. The bars can be refrigerated for up to 4 days or frozen for up to 2 months.

banana brulée ultimate sundae for two

Enjoy an easy dessert with these full-custom, hot-rod banana splits. You could also make mini splits with tropical baby bananas sliced in half lengthwise and caramelized. Or take things Latin with a cinnamon-chocolate ice cream and warmed dulce de leche or cajeta instead of traditional hot fudge and strawberries.

prep time: 10 minutes | *yields:* 2 servings

Sprinkle the brown sugar on a saucer. Dip one cut side of each banana slice in the brown sugar and place the slices, sugar-side up, on a baking sheet. Using a kitchen torch, heat the sugar until it melts and begins to caramelize. Alternatively, if you don't have a kitchen torch, place the bananas under the broiler for just a few minutes. Watch carefully, as the sugar can burn quickly.

Place the ice cream scoops in a large shallow dessert bowl and top with the warmed caramel and hot fudge sauce. Add the bananas, strawberries, and nuts. Garnish with mint leaves and serve immediately with two spoons.

ingredients

1 tablespoon packed light brown sugar

1 large banana, cut diagonally into 1-inch-thick slices

2 scoops vanilla ice cream

2 tablespoons store-bought caramel sauce, warmed

2 tablespoons store-bought hot fudge sauce, warmed

¼ cup sliced fresh strawberries

2 tablespoons chopped almonds or other nuts

Mint leaves for garnish

variations

Other ice creams like pralines-and-cream, cinnamon, or butter pecan would be good.

gingersnap cheesecake
with caramel walnut sauce

This beautiful winter dessert makes enough for the two of you and just enough leftovers. For a change from the Caramel Walnut Sauce, sprinkle extra crushed gingersnaps over the top for added gingery crunch and spoon with warmed apricot preserves for over-the-top richness.

ingredients

prep time: 25 minutes | *baking & chilling:* 3 hours | *yields:* 6 servings

crust

16 gingersnaps or vanilla wafers, crushed

4 tablespoons (½ stick) unsalted butter, melted

cheesecake

3 large eggs

6 tablespoons honey

2 teaspoons vanilla extract

1 tablespoon cornstarch

2 (8-ounce) packages cream cheese

1 cup sour cream

topping

½ cup store-bought caramel sauce

½ cup walnut halves

variations

Try chocolate cookies in place of the gingersnaps, and a fresh raspberry sauce instead of the caramel and walnuts.

Preheat the oven to 350 degrees. Line the bottom and sides of a 6-inch springform pan with parchment paper.

To make the crust, place the crushed cookies and butter in a small bowl, stirring to combine. Press into the bottom of the prepared springform pan with clean hands.

For the cheesecake, combine the eggs, honey, vanilla, and cornstarch in a medium bowl and whisk until combined. Add the cream cheese and sour cream, whisking until smooth. Spoon the mixture over the cookie base and bake for 40 minutes, or until set. To test for perfect doneness, tap on the side of the pan with a large spoon. The cheesecake is cooked through when the center does not wobble independently of the sides. Let the cheesecake cool to room temperature, and then chill for 2 hours.

To unmold the cheesecake, cover the top of the cheesecake with a piece of parchment or wax paper and place a plate upside-down on top. Holding the plate and cake together, turn both over so that the plate is on the bottom. Release the sides from the springform pan and carefully remove. Remove the bottom of the springform pan. Peel off the parchment paper. Place a serving plate upside down on the crust of the cheesecake and flip over. Remove the wax paper.

For the topping, warm the caramel sauce and stir in the walnuts. Drizzle over the cake before serving.

chocolate ganache cake with sugared rose petals

If you've somehow lived your life without having a cake frosted with ganache, now's your chance to make up for it. You'll wonder why you ever bothered with buttercream. The fudge-like consistency and concentrated chocolate is a very simple process, yet a knockout result—especially with the brightly colored rose petals for extra decoration. While the recipe may seem a bit labor-intensive, it's perfect for two sweet-tooths in the kitchen: one of you can work on the cake, while the other focuses on the filling. Just try to keep your fingers out of each other's bowl!

prep time: 55 minutes | *cooking & cooling:* 3½ hours | *yields:* 8 servings

Preheat the oven to 325 degrees. Spray two 8-inch round cake pans with nonstick cooking spray. Line the bottoms of the pans with parchment paper and spray the paper with nonstick cooking spray.

To make the cake, sift the flour, baking powder, baking soda, and salt together in a medium bowl. Place the chocolate morsels in a microwave-safe glass container. Microwave on high at 20-second intervals, stirring between each interval until the chocolate is melted and completely smooth.

Cream the brown sugar, butter, and vanilla in a large bowl with an electric mixer. (The mixture will be dry.) Add the eggs, 1 at a time, beating well after each addition. Beat in the melted chocolate. Add half the dry ingredients and all the buttermilk. Mix until combined. Add the remaining dry ingredients and mix until incorporated. Divide the batter evenly between the prepared pans.

Bake until a toothpick inserted into center comes out clean, about 22 minutes. Remove from the oven and place the cake pans on a wire rack to cool. After 30 minutes, turn the cakes out onto the rack and peel off the parchment. Slice the tops off the cakes, if necessary, for a level surface. You can make the cakes up to a day ahead up to this point. Wrap in plastic and store at room temperature until ready to frost. Alternatively, you can freeze the cakes for up to 1 month.

(continued)

ingredients

cake

	Nonstick cooking spray
1	cup all-purpose flour
½	teaspoon baking powder
½	teaspoon baking soda
½	teaspoon kosher salt
6	ounces semisweet chocolate morsels (1 cup)
1¼	cups packed light brown sugar
4	tablespoons (½ stick) unsalted butter, room temperature
1	teaspoon vanilla extract
2	large eggs
½	cup buttermilk

filling

1	cup heavy cream
1	tablespoon confectioners' sugar
3	tablespoons sweetened cocoa powder

ganache

8	ounces good-quality dark chocolate, chopped
2	tablespoons unsalted butter, room temperature
¾	cup heavy cream

chocolate ganache cake with sugared rose petals (continued)

rose petals

12 organic edible rose petals
or other edible flowers

2 tablespoons pasteurized
egg whites

3 tablespoons granulated sugar

variations

Save time by using a boxed chocolate cake mix and preparing the filling and toppings by hand. Garnish with chocolate curls by "peeling" a room-temperature chocolate bar with a vegetable peeler, or with chopped walnuts instead of petals.

Wrap them in plastic and then in aluminum foil. Place in a resealable plastic bag and store in the freezer until ready to use. Thaw, unwrapped, to room temperature before frosting.

To prepare the filling, place the cream, confectioners' sugar, and cocoa powder in large bowl and beat with an electric mixer until stiff peaks form. Cover and chill until ready to use.

Cut a piece of cardboard in a circle the same size as the cake bottom. Place one cake on the cardboard. Spread all the cream filling over the top of the cake. Cover loosely with plastic wrap and refrigerate for an hour. Reserve the remaining cake to stack once the filling is firmer.

To make the ganache, place the chopped chocolate and butter in a medium bowl. Heat the cream in a small, heavy saucepan over medium heat. Bring just to a boil and remove from heat. Pour over the chocolate and let stand for 5 minutes. Stir until the chocolate has melted and the mixture is smooth.

Remove the cake from the refrigerator and top with the remaining cake layer. Place the stacked cake on a wire rack set over a baking sheet. Pour half of the ganache over the top and sides of cake and refrigerate for 30 minutes.

Heat the remaining ganache in small saucepan over very low heat, stirring constantly. Pour the remaining ganache over the chilled cake, spreading to cover the top and sides. Chill until the ganache has set, about 30 minutes. The cake can be made a day ahead to this point if kept refrigerated.

To make the sugared flowers, beat the egg whites with a fork until slightly foamy. Brush the petals on all sides with the beaten egg whites and sprinkle with the sugar. Set on a wire rack or wax paper to dry. Store the sugared flowers in an airtight container until ready to garnish the cake.

old-fashioned sugar cookies

Eating one of these classic cookies is like biting into buttery heaven. They make fantastic ice cream sandwiches. This recipe makes enough dough for three dozen cookies, but when it's just the two of us, I bake one dozen and freeze the rest of the dough. (It will keep for a month wrapped tightly in plastic wrap and then aluminum foil.) When your sweet tooth strikes, simply slice off enough cookies from the frozen dough for you and your honey, and bake until light golden.

prep time: 20 minutes	*baking & chilling:* 45 minutes	*yields:* 3 dozen

Cream the butter, oil, granulated sugar, and confectioners' sugar in a medium bowl with an electric mixer until well blended. Add the egg and vanilla, and continue beating until well combined.

Sift together the flour, baking soda, cream of tartar, and salt in a medium bowl. Stir in the lemon zest. Add to the butter mixture, ½ cup at a time, beating after each addition until thoroughly mixed.

Remove the dough from the bowl and place on a sheet of wax paper in the form of a log. Begin rolling the wax paper around the log, and continue rolling back and forth against the work surface to form a clean, even log about 9 inches long and 2 inches in diameter. Roll completely up in the wax paper and twist tightly at the ends. Refrigerate until firm, at least 30 minutes. (The dough can be stored in the refrigerator for up to 3 days or in the freezer for up to 1 month. For freezing or longer refrigeration, wrap the log directly in plastic wrap and then again in aluminum foil to keep the dough from drying out.)

Preheat the oven to 350 degrees. Spray two large baking sheets with nonstick cooking spray.

Unwrap the log of dough and slice into ¼-inch circles using a long, sharp knife. (Unflavored dental floss also slices through dough cleanly.) To help the cookies keep their shape, cut with a sawing motion instead of pressing down through the dough. Place the cookies on the prepared pans and sprinkle with the granulated sugar. Bake until light-golden brown, about 12 to 15 minutes. (Frozen dough can be baked as well— just add 1 to 2 minutes to the baking time.) Transfer to wire racks with a thin spatula and cool completely before storing in an airtight container.

ingredients

- 8 tablespoons (1 stick) unsalted butter, room temperature
- ½ cup canola or vegetable oil
- ½ cup granulated sugar, plus more for sprinkling
- ½ cup confectioners' sugar
- 1 large egg
- 1 teaspoon vanilla extract
- 2¼ cups all-purpose flour, plus more for dusting
- ½ teaspoon baking soda
- ½ teaspoon cream of tartar
- ½ teaspoon kosher salt
- 2 tablespoons finely grated lemon zest
- Nonstick cooking spray for greasing

variations

Roll the log of dough in colored sugar crystals, finely chopped nuts, or cinnamon sugar before wrapping in wax paper and chilling.

fresh fruit with mascarpone

Try this light, elegant finale when you've spent your calorie budget on a much richer main course. Mascarpone is an Italian cheese with a very smooth texture and slightly sweet-fresh flavor. It will leave you feeling sated but not stuffed—and ready for after-dinner adventure.

ingredients

8 ounces mascarpone cheese
1 tablespoon heavy cream
2 tablespoons honey
2 nectarines, sliced
½ cup blackberries
½ cup blueberries
½ cup raspberries
   Mint sprigs for garnish

variations

Use yogurt or crème fraîche in lieu of mascarpone, and gently flavor it with fresh vanilla or almond extract.

prep time: 10 minutes | *yields:* 4 servings

Whisk together the mascarpone, cream, and honey in a small bowl until thoroughly mixed and creamy. Cover and chill until ready to use.

Arrange the fruit in 4 dessert glasses or shallow dessert bowls along with a large spoonful of mascarpone. Garnish with mint and serve cold.

rosemary-orange crème brulée

This silky, sexy dessert is perfect for date night. I like to make the custard, and Fritz loves to fire up his propane torch and caramelize the sugar on top. To test custards for doneness, gently tap the side of the baking dish or slightly shake the pan and watch to see how the contents jiggle. The center of the custard should barely jiggle independently of the sides. The custard can be made the day before and refrigerated, but save the caramelizing until you're ready to serve.

ingredients

1½ cups heavy cream

1   vanilla bean

1   (4-inch) sprig rosemary

9   large egg yolks

6   tablespoons granulated sugar

2   teaspoons finely grated
     orange zest (about ½ orange)

2   tablespoons packed
     light brown sugar

variations

Lend a delicate flavor with a teaspoon of orange or rose water, and garnish with an orange blossom. Or replace the orange zest with lemon and the rosemary with lavender.

prep time: 25 minutes | *cooking & chilling:* 3 hours | *yields:* 6 servings

Preheat the oven to 325 degrees. Bring a teapot or large saucepan of water to a boil for the *bain-marie*, or water bath, for baking the brulées. Reduce the heat to low to keep the water hot until ready to use.

Pour the cream into a heavy, medium saucepan. Split the vanilla bean pod in half lengthwise. Use the edge of your knife to scrape the seeds from the bean. Add the seeds and the pod to the cream, along with the sprig of rosemary. Set the pan over medium heat and bring just to a simmer for the flavors to infuse the cream. Watch carefully so that cream does not boil, and remove from the heat when it reaches a simmer.

Prepare a medium double-boiler or find a medium, heat-safe mixing bowl that fits comfortably in a saucepan. Fill the bottom of the double-boiler with enough water so that it comes close, but does not touch, the top pan or mixing bowl. Set over high heat and bring to a boil.

Reduce the heat to a simmer and set the top of the double-boiler over the simmering water. Add the egg yolks and granulated sugar. Whisk constantly until the yolk mixture is pale yellow and hot to the touch, about 3 minutes. Be very careful not to let any water get into the yolk mixture.

Remove the vanilla pod and rosemary sprig from the cream and discard. Gradually whisk the hot cream mixture into the egg yolk mixture, adding the hot cream slowly so the egg yolks do not curdle. Stir in the orange zest.

rosemary-orange crème brulée *(continued)*

Pour the mixture evenly among six (6-ounce) ramekins. Place the ramekins in a large baking dish. Set the dish in the oven and pour enough of the hot water (from the teapot or saucepan) to come halfway up the sides of the ramekins, being careful not to splash any water into the custards. Bake until the custard is almost set in the center and light golden on top, about 35 minutes. Remove the custards from the water bath and refrigerate until chilled, at least 2 hours or overnight.

Sprinkle a teaspoon of brown sugar on each custard. Heat the sugar with a kitchen torch until it melts and turns dark brown, about 1 minute each. If you don't have a kitchen torch, place the ramekins on a baking sheet and place under the broiler until the sugar just starts to melt, rotating the baking sheet so that tops brown evenly. In either case, watch the sugar carefully, as it can turn from golden brown to burnt in a flash. Serve immediately.

lemon bars

My grandfather was a sucker for lemon bars, and I suspect that your date will find himself equally enamored. The lemon is tart without too much acidity, but still has a good sweet bite. When the weather is particularly nice, we love to pack a picnic basket and take it down to the beach for a scenic lunch by the water. These old-fashioned lemon bars travel well, so we often nestle a few into our cooler and bring them along.

prep time: 15 minutes | *baking & chilling:* 1½ hours | *yields:* 12 pieces

Preheat the oven to 350 degrees.

For the cookie base, sift together the flour, salt, and confectioners' sugar in large bowl. Cut the butter into ½-inch pieces. Add to the flour mixture and cut in with a pastry cutter or with 2 knives until the mixture resembles coarse meal. Press the mixture into the bottom of a 9 x 9 x 2-inch baking dish. Bake until light-golden brown, about 20 minutes. Remove from the oven and set on a wire rack, but leave the oven on.

While the cookie base is baking, combine the eggs, granulated sugar, lemon juice, flour, and lemon zest with an electric mixer in medium bowl. Pour the egg mixture on top of the warm crust. Return the pan to the oven and bake until the lemon mixture has set, about 20 minutes. Let cool completely before cutting into 12 bars. Sift the confectioners' sugar over the top of each bar before serving.

ingredients

base

- 1½ cups all purpose flour
- ⅛ teaspoon salt
- ⅓ cup confectioners' sugar
- 12 tablespoons (1½ sticks) unsalted butter, chilled

topping

- 3 large eggs
- 1½ cups granulated sugar
- ⅓ cup freshly squeezed lemon juice (about 2 medium lemons)
- 3 tablespoons all-purpose flour
- 1 tablespoon finely grated lemon zest (about 1½ medium lemons)
- 2 tablespoons confectioners' sugar for dusting

variations

Replace traditional lemons with Meyer lemons for a sweeter bar. Or, replace half of the lemon juice with lime, tangerine, or orange juice to lessen the tartness as well. Press ½ cup of shredded coconut into the pastry base before baking.

spiced mexican wedding cookies

If you're not ready to talk to your honey about the m-word, you can just call these Mexican Spice Cookies. They're incredibly easy, so you can make them on a night when you're spending a lot of time and effort on the main course. Lick off any errant powdered sugar from your hands.

prep time: 20 minutes | *baking & chilling:* 1 hour | *yields:* 4 dozen

Place the butter in large mixing bowl and beat with an electric mixer until light and fluffy. Sift in 1 cup of the confectioners' sugar, the cinnamon, and cloves. Add the vanilla, and continue mixing until well blended. Add the flour, 1/2 cup at a time, beating until well incorporated. Mix in the pecans and candied ginger, if using.

Divide the dough in half and form into 2 balls; flatten slightly. Wrap each ball tightly in plastic wrap and chill until cold, about 30 minutes. (The dough can be frozen at this point for up to 1 month.)

Preheat the oven to 350 degrees. Place the remaining confectioners' sugar in a medium bowl.

Roll the dough into 1-inch balls and arrange on a baking sheet an inch apart (they won't spread very much). Bake 16 to 18 minutes, or until the cookies are golden brown on the bottom and just slightly golden on top. Let cool for a few minutes on the baking sheet, and then gently toss in the confectioners' sugar, coating completely. Place the cookies on a wire rack to cool completely before storing in an airtight container.

ingredients

- 16 tablespoons (2 sticks) unsalted butter, room temperature
- 2 cups confectioners' sugar, divided
- 1/4 teaspoon ground cinnamon
- 1/8 teaspoon ground cloves
- 2 teaspoons vanilla extract
- 2 cups all-purpose flour
- 1 cup finely chopped pecans, toasted
- 1/4 cup minced candied ginger (optional)

variations

Instead of rolling these in confectioners' sugar, dip them in cocoa powder or melted high-quality dark chocolate.

almond-pear galette

A galette is a rustic, free-form pie—so rustic, you don't even need a pie pan! If you don't have the time (or the inclination) to make the crust from scratch, substitute a prepared pie crust. Look for the frozen crust that comes rolled in a box, not the kind that's already in a pie tin, and save your energy for enjoying this fruit dessert. You don't have to stick with just one kind of fruit for the filling—mix whatever is in season and of similar textures so that they will bake evenly. Try apples and plums.

ingredients

prep time: 45 minutes | *baking & chilling:* 2 hours | *yields:* 6-8 servings

pastry

- 1¼ cups all-purpose flour, plus more for dusting
- 2 tablespoons sugar
- ¼ teaspoon baking powder
- ¼ teaspoon kosher salt
- ⅛ teaspoon baking soda
- 5 tablespoons cold, unsalted butter, cut into ½-inch cubes and chilled
- ¼ cup plus 2 tablespoons cultured buttermilk
- ¼ teaspoon pure almond extract

almond paste

- 4 tablespoons (½ stick) unsalted butter, room temperature
- ¼ cup sugar
- 1 large egg plus 1 large egg white
- ⅓ cup almond meal or finely ground almonds
- ¼ teaspoon pure almond extract
- 1 tablespoon dark rum

To make the pastry, place the flour, sugar, baking powder, salt, and baking soda in the bowl of a food processor and pulse just to combine. Add the butter and pulse until the butter pieces are the size of small peas and the mixture resembles coarse meal. Combine the buttermilk and almond extract in a measuring cup. Add the buttermilk mixture to the pastry mixture a little at a time and pulse just until the dough comes together. Form the dough into a disk and dust lightly with flour. Wrap in plastic wrap and refrigerate for 1 hour.

To make the almond paste, beat the butter and sugar together in a medium bowl with an electric mixer on medium speed until the butter lightens in color. Add the egg and egg white, and continue beating on a lower speed until the mixture becomes light and fluffy, 4 to 5 minutes. Beat in the almond meal, almond extract, and rum. Cover with plastic wrap and refrigerate until ready to use.

To make the filling, peel and core the pears. Cut into ¼-inch-thick slices and toss together with the lemon juice and zest to help keep them from oxidizing and turning brown.

Heat the oven to 400 degrees and line a large baking sheet with a piece of parchment. Set another piece of parchment on your work surface and dust lightly with flour. Remove the refrigerated dough from the plastic wrap and place on the parchment. Lightly dust the dough with more flour and top with another sheet of parchment. *(continued)*

almond-pear galette *(continued)*

Roll out the dough, turning and rolling until you have a rustic circle about 12 inches in diameter. Peel off the top layer of the parchment. Invert the dough onto the parchment-lined baking sheet.

Spread the almond paste over the dough, leaving a 1-inch border. Arrange the pear slices in concentric circles over the paste. Sprinkle with the sugar and cinnamon. Fold the edges of dough over the pears, crimping the dough to enclose the edges of the pears. Scatter the bits of butter over the top.

Bake the galette for 20 to 25 minutes, or until the pears are tender and the crust is golden brown. If the edges of the crust are browning too fast, cover with a sheet of aluminum foil. Remove from the oven and let cool on the baking sheet for 5 minutes. Transfer the parchment and galette to a wire rack, and let cool completely. Cut into wedges and serve.

filling

3	firm but ripe Anjou or Bartlett pears
2	tablespoons freshly squeezed lemon juice (about 1 small lemon)
1½	teaspoons freshly grated lemon zest (about 1 small lemon)
¼	cup sugar
¼	teaspoon cinnamon
1	tablespoon unsalted butter, cut into small pieces and chilled

variations

Drizzle a little warm caramel sauce over the galette before serving. Whip a cup of heavy cream with 2 tablespoons of sugar and a tablespoon of liqueur to serve as a garnish.

peanut butter-chocolate ganache bars

Think peanut butter cups, only much, much better. Just read the ingredients list and you'll know exactly what I mean. Don't skimp on the dark chocolate when it comes to quality—this ganache will be the crowning jewel to the peanut-buttery base.

prep time: 12 minutes | *cooking & cooling:* 2 hours | *yields:* 32 pieces

Line an 8- or 9-inch square cake pan with wax paper.

For the base, combine the brown sugar, confectioners' sugar, peanut butter, and butter in a medium bowl. Stir in the graham cracker crumbs. Press into bottom of the prepared cake pan with clean hands.

To make the ganache, place the cream in a small, heavy saucepan set over medium-high heat, and bring just to a boil. Remove from the heat and add the chocolate. Allow the chocolate to sit in the hot cream for a few minutes, and then stir until the chocolate is melted and the mixture is mooth. Add the butter, stirring until smooth.

Pour the ganache over the peanut butter mixture and refrigerate until chocolate is firm enough to cut, about 2 hours. Cut into 1 x 2-inch pieces. Tightly cover with plastic wrap, and store in the refrigerator for up to 1 week or in the freezer for up to 2 months.

ingredients

peanut-butter base

- ¼ cup packed light brown sugar
- 1½ cups confectioners' sugar
- ¾ cup smooth peanut butter
- 4 tablespoons unsalted butter, room temperature
- ½ cup graham cracker crumbs

chocolate ganache

- 8 ounces good-quality dark chocolate, chopped
- ¾ cup heavy cream
- 2 tablespoons unsalted butter, room temperature

variations

Sprinkle the ganache with roasted and salted peanuts before chilling. Make in foil cupcake liners and peel away for a homemade Reese's effect.

red wine-poached pears

This elegant dessert is deceptively simple. Serve the pears chilled in a small pool of chilled Whipped Cream (page 151) or warm Marsala Zabaglione (page 155) for a luscious yet light finale. In wintry months, skip the pears altogether and serve the warmed poaching liquid as mulled wine.

ingredients

| prep & cooking time: 1 hour | chilling: overnight | yields: 4 servings |

4   firm but ripe Bosc or
    Anjou pears

1   (750-ml) bottle Merlot

1   cup plus 2 tablespoons
    sugar, divided

1   cup water

2   teaspoons vanilla extract

1   stick cinnamon

4   whole cloves
    Ground cinnamon for garnish

variations

Use white wine and add cherries, or try using a sweet white dessert wine and elimating half the sugar. Garnish with toasted or candied chopped pecans.

Peel the pears, leaving a bit of skin and the stem intact at the top.

Combine the wine, 1 cup of the sugar, the water, vanilla, cinnamon, and cloves in large, heavy saucepan over medium-high heat. Bring to a boil, stirring frequently until the sugar dissolves. Add the pears, reduce the heat, and cover. Simmer until the pears are tender when pierced with knife, but not too soft—about 15 minutes. Remove from the heat and allow the pears to cool completely in the wine mixture. Cover and chill the pears in the liquid overnight.

Remove the pears from the liquid and keep chilled until ready to serve. Remove the cloves and cinnamon stick and discard. Return the liquid to the stovetop and bring to a boil over medium-high heat. Let boil until the liquid has reduced to a syrupy consistency, about 30 minutes. Remove from the heat and let cool at least 30 to 45 minutes before serving.

Serve the chilled pears with the syrup and some creamy sweetened mascarpone (page 134), Whipped Cream (page 151), or the Marsala Zabaglione (page 155). Sprinkle with ground cinnamon for garnish.

whipped cream

ingredients

- 1 cup (½ pint) heavy whipping cream, chilled
- 2 tablespoons sugar, preferably superfine, or more to taste
- ¼ teaspoon vanilla extract

variations

Flavor the cream with one of these additions to better accent your dessert: add 1 teaspoon espresso powder or 1 tablespoon instant coffee granules; 1 tablespoon cocoa powder; 1 teaspoon cinnamon; or 1 tablespoon of your favorite liqueur. Try different extracts like peppermint or almond. Use brown sugar, pure maple syrup, or fruit jams instead of white sugar.

prep time: 5 minutes | *yields:* 2 cups

Chill a large mixing bowl and the beaters from an electric mixer (or whisk) in the freezer or refrigerator. Add the chilled cream to the chilled bowl and beat on low speed until the cream begins to form little bubbles. (Or whisk by hand.) Continue beating until the cream begins to get foamy.

Sprinkle in the sugar, vanilla, and any additional flavors. Increase the speed to medium, and beat to incorporate. The beaters will make "tracks" in the cream.

Increase the speed to high and beat until the cream has nearly doubled in size and forms stiff peaks. Be careful not to overbeat—stopping sooner rather than later—as the cream will turn grainy and start to turn to butter.

If not serving immediately, pour into a fine sieve and suspend in the mixing bowl. Cover with plastic wrap and refrigerate for up to 8 hours.

blueberry sorbet

In the heat of summer, homemade sorbet is deliciously refreshing. The alcohol will keep the sorbet from freezing into a solid block, and the frozen berries help to cut down on the chilling time. Keep excess berries in the freezer so that you can use well-ripened fruit every time, even in the winter. Make all of the sorbets and serve a small scoop of each for a beautiful spectrum of colors.

ingredients

1½ pounds frozen blueberries

¾ cup sugar, or more if desired

¼ cup Cabernet Sauvignon

variations

Try frozen blackberries and wildflower honey instead of blueberries and sugar.

prep time: 5 minutes	chilling time: 60 minutes	yields: 3 cups

Combine all the ingredients in the bowl of a food processor and blend until smooth. Taste and add more sugar if the mixture seems too tart. Place the sorbet in an airtight container and freeze until firm before serving, at least 1 hour.

mango sorbet

Try this mango sorbet after a hearty meal like my Lamb Vindaloo (page 111). The texture of the fruit lends a silkiness to an otherwise icy dessert. If you like, you can add a little ground cardamom to the mixture.

ingredients

1½ pounds frozen mango pieces (about 3 or 4 mangoes)

¾ cup sugar

2 tablespoons light rum

2 tablespoons water

variations

Try frozen pineapple in addition to the mango, or a combination of pineapple and sweetened, shredded coconut.

prep time: 5 minutes	chilling time: 60 minutes	yields: 3 cups

If using fresh mango, freeze the chopped mango for at least 1 hour before using. Combine the frozen mango, sugar, rum, and water in the bowl of a food processor. Blend until the mixture is smooth. Place the sorbet in an airtight container and freeze until firm before serving, at least 1 hour.

grapefruit sorbet

Try making this sorbet in winter, when grapefruit are in season and you're looking for a light finish to a heavy meal or a palate cleanser between courses. Regular grapefruit yields a nearly white sorbet, and ruby-red grapefruit makes pale pink. In the summer, you can mix slightly softened sorbet with vodka for a frozen Greyhound cocktail.

ingredients

- 4 cups grapefruit segments, drained and frozen (about 3 medium grapefruit)
- 1 cup sugar
- 3 tablespoons vodka

variations

Add 1 to 2 tablespoons super-finely minced candied ginger for a bit of spice or minced tarragon for an herbal note.

prep time: 5 minutes | **chilling time:** 60 minutes | **yields:** 4 cups

For a quick-and-easy dessert, buy the pre-cut, already-segmented grapefruit sections in the refrigerated section of your grocer's produce department. If they don't carry the pre-cut grapefruit, you can do it yourself. Using a sharp knife, cut the ends off the grapefruit so they can sit without rolling. Working from top to bottom, cut off the peel and white pith from the fruit. Working over a large bowl to catch the juice, use a sharp knife to cut in between each membrane to free the grapefruit segments. Discard any seeds. Freeze the grapefruit segments and juice for at least 1 hour.

Combine the frozen grapefruit sections, sugar, and vodka in the bowl of a food processor. Blend until the mixture is smooth. Place the sorbet in an airtight container and freeze until firm before serving, at least 1 hour.

raspberry sorbet

In the late summer and early fall, many raspberry growers open their fields for visitors to pick their own berries. Plan a day trip to pick raspberries for a romantic date, though you may be tempted to indulge in the fruits of your labor before you even make it home. The addition of vodka gives this dessert a grown-up edge, and the berries keep things sweet in this ruby-red sorbet.

ingredients

- 1½ pounds frozen raspberries
- ¾ cup sugar
- 2 tablespoons vodka
- 2 tablespoons water

variations

Use frozen strawberries or cherries in place of the raspberry. Try cognac in place of the vodka.

prep time: 5 minutes | **chilling time:** 60 minutes | **yields:** 3 cups

Combine all the ingredients in the bowl of a food processor and blend until smooth. Place the sorbet in an airtight container and freeze until firm before serving, at least 1 hour.

marsala zabaglione

I can't refuse this light whipped custard when it's on a dessert menu. At home you can spoon it over fresh fruit or serve it with hazelnut cookies bought at an Italian bakery. The secret to making the zabaglione is to not let it get too hot or the eggs will curdle. Because the eggs don't get fully cooked, you might want to buy pasteurized eggs. Look for them in upscale grocery stores.

prep time: 6 minutes | *cooking time:* 10 minutes | *yields:* 4 servings

Prepare a large double-boiler or find a large mixing bowl that fits comfortably in a large saucepan. Fill the bottom of the double-boiler with enough water so that it comes close, but does not touch the top pan or mixing bowl. Set over high heat and bring to a boil.

While the water is coming to a boil, combine the yolks, sugar, and wine in the top of the double-boiler or a mixing bowl set on your work surface. Beat the ingredients with an electric mixer on high speed until foamy. Reduce the water to a simmer and set the yolk mixture over the simmering water. Continue beating; the mixture will thicken and increase greatly in volume. When the mixture is thick, foamy, and warm to the touch, pour into dessert glasses. Serve the warm custard immediately. Top with fresh berries for color and serve with tuiles for crunch.

ingredients

4 large egg yolks, room temperature

½ cup sugar

½ cup Marsala wine

Fresh berries for garnish

Store-bought tuiles for garnish

variations

Make a quick trifle with a layer of ladyfingers, a layer of custard, and a layer of berries in a cocktail glass. Garnish with mint.

pumpkin wontons
with brown butter-walnut sauce

Some nights you feel like taking a wild leap and trying something you've never done before.
These pumpkin wontons are for one of those nights. This is a totally original preparation, and
it's easier than you think. Canned pumpkin works perfectly well and keeps things simple.
Serve with a big scoop of vanilla ice cream.

prep time: 20 minutes | *cooking time:* 15 minutes | *yields:* 16 wontons

Combine the pumpkin, egg, brown sugar, flour, nutmeg, cinnamon, and ginger in a small bowl, and mix well. Place a rounded teaspoon of the pumpkin mixture in the center of each wonton wrapper. Dampen the edges of each wrapper with a little water and fold in half diagonally to form a triangle, pinching to seal. (The wontons can be made up to this point a day in advance, covered, and refrigerated until ready to fry. They can also be frozen: Place the wontons in an individual layer on a baking sheet and freeze. Transfer the wontons to a heavy-duty, resealable plastic bag and store in the freezer until ready to fry.)

Set a small, heavy saucepan over medium-low heat and add the butter and brown sugar. Stir occasionally until the sugar has dissolved, about 7 minutes. Stir in the walnuts and remove from the heat.

Set some paper towels on your workspace for draining the fried wontons. Pour enough oil to come 1 inch up the sides of a medium saucepan and set over medium-high heat. Pinch off a bit of extra wonton and drop in the oil to test. When the oil begins to sizzle (about 350 degrees), fry the wontons in batches until golden brown, about 2 to 3 minutes. Place on the paper towels to drain.

Place a scoop of ice cream in shallow dessert bowls. Spoon with the walnut sauce and wedge 1 or 2 wontons into the ice cream. Serve immediately, while the ice cream is cold and the wontons are hot.

ingredients

wontons

½ cup cooked, puréed pumpkin or canned pumpkin

1 large egg

2 tablespoons packed brown sugar

2 tablespoons all-purpose flour

⅛ teaspoon freshly grated nutmeg

⅛ teaspoon ground cinnamon

Pinch of ground ginger

16 wonton wrappers

Canola or vegetable oil for frying

sauce

8 tablespoons (1 stick) unsalted butter

¼ cup packed brown sugar

⅓ cup coarsely chopped walnuts

Vanilla ice cream for serving

variations

For alternate fillings, try cream cheese and fruit jam, chopped dried fruit soaked in brandy, or chopped fresh fruit sprinkled with brown sugar and tapioca.

chocolate amaretto truffles

These chocolate truffles deliver the intensely rich chocolate kick we all crave, and it's fun to make them together. With so few ingredients, the quality really matters here. I love Scharffen Berger cocoa powder and chocolates like El Rey, Michel Cluizel, and Callebaut. You can also dip these beautiful candies in melted chocolate and roll in chopped nuts or chocolate shavings, as we did in the photograph.

ingredients

12 ounces good-quality dark chocolate, chopped

¾ cup heavy cream

1 tablespoon amaretto or other liqueur (optional)

¼ cup unsweetened cocoa powder

variations

Replace the amaretto with other liqueurs: Kirsch for a cherry flavor, Kahlúa for coffee, or Cointreau for orange.

prep time: 5 minutes | *cooking & chilling:* 3-4 hours | *yields:* 32 pieces

Line a rimmed baking sheet with wax paper. Place the chopped chocolate in the bowl of a food processor. Heat the cream in a small saucepan on medium-high until just boiling. Pour the hot cream over the chocolate. Let stand for 1 minute, and then process until smooth. Add the liqueur, if using, and process to mix well.

Pour the chocolate mixture into a shallow bowl and cool for 20 minutes. Cover with plastic wrap and refrigerate until firm, 2 or 3 hours.

Scoop about 2 teaspoons of chocolate mixture and form into irregular ball shapes for a rustic look. Place on the prepared baking sheet and repeat with the remaining chocolate mixture. Refrigerate the truffles for 30 minutes to re-set.

Place the cocoa powder in a small bowl and toss each truffle in the cocoa powder to coat. Store in an airtight container in the refrigerator for up to 2 weeks.

chapter six

drinks

What better way to relax after a
long day and ease yourself into
the dinner hour than with
a round of cocktails? When
you want to move beyond
traditional well drinks,
try one of these easy
but exotic libations.

frosted black-and-cream

Use espresso, root beer, or cream soda in place of the Guinness® for this innovative ice cream float. Top with crushed biscotti or cookies.

yields: 2 drinks

2   tablespoons turbinado sugar
4   scoops vanilla ice cream
1   (16-ounce) can Guinness® or
    other stout beer, chilled

Chill 2 tall beer or shake glasses for 10 minutes in the freezer. Sprinkle the turbinado sugar in a saucer. Moisten the rim of each glass and dip in the turbinado to coat. Place 2 scoops of ice cream in each glass and fill with the chilled beer. Serve immediately with a long spoon and a straw.

simple syrup

When making cocktails, use simple syrup in lieu of sugar for sweetening. Unlike granulated sugar, it will mix instantly with the cocktail for perfectly sweet results. Have fun infusing the syrup with any variety of herbs or spices like mint, rosemary, ginger, Earl Grey, cardamom, or vanilla for unexpected tastes. Strain the flavoring agent from the syrup before storing.

1   cup sugar
1   cup water

Combine the sugar and water in a small saucepan over medium heat, and stir until the sugar dissolves. Increase the heat to a boil, and then reduce the heat to a simmer for 3 minutes. Let the syrup cool completely, and then transfer to an airtight container. It will keep in the refrigerator for up to 2 weeks.

frozen pomegranate margaritas

The deep red color of this drink may remind you of a virgin strawberry daiquiri, but this is definitely a cocktail for grown-ups. The sweet/tart flavor of pomegranate juice (which you can also find blended with blueberry, cherry, mango, and tangerine juices) is more refined than any blender drink you've ever had.

yields: 4 drinks

8 ounces (1 cup) premium tequila
2 ounces (¼ cup) triple sec
4 ounces (½ cup) freshly squeezed lime juice, 5 or 6 medium limes
2 ounces (¼ cup) pomegranate juice
Lime slices for garnish

Chill four margarita glasses in the freezer for at least 10 minutes.

Pour the tequila, triple sec, lime juice, and pomegranate juice into the pitcher of a blender. Fill the pitcher with ice and blend until smooth. Pour the mixture into the glasses and garnish with lime slices. Serve immediately.

passion fruit martini

Beauty is in the eye of the beholder. If you can get past the unfortunate exterior appearance of the passion fruit, you'll find an exotic, distinctly tropical aroma. Never mind its yellow or purply wrinkled skin, this fruit is a testament to not judging a book by its cover and finding inner sweetness where you least expect it.

yields: 1 drink

2 ounces (¼ cup) chilled vodka
2 ounces (¼ cup) passion fruit liqueur (such as Alizé)
Lime slices for garnish

Chill a martini glass in the freezer for at least 10 minutes. Fill a cocktail shaker with ice and add the vodka and passion fruit liqueur. Shake for 30 seconds, and then strain the mixture into the chilled glass. Garnish with a lime and serve immediately.

white orchid

Lychees grow all over Southeast Asia, where they are often combined with sugar and water for a refreshing afternoon drink. They have a pebbled pinky-red skin and a white orb of flesh that's almost the texture of a grape. Fully ripe, they are bite-size bursts of sweetness. This cocktail captures that flavor and adds a kick with the effervescence of Champagne. For a really special night, garnish the drinks with fresh orchids.

yields: 2 drinks

1   (15-ounce) can lychees in syrup
2   ounces (4 tablespoons) vodka
1   (750-ml) bottle Champagne or
    other sparkling wine, chilled
    Fresh orchids for garnish (optional)

Chill two tall glasses in the freezer for at least 10 minutes.

Place 4 to 6 lychees in the bottom of each glass. Pour 1 teaspoon of their syrup over them.

Add 1 ounce of vodka to each glass, then fill the glasses with crushed ice. Pour in enough Champagne to fill the glasses to the top, garnish with a fresh orchid, and serve immediately.

peach sangria

This is a lighter, more elegant version of the classic Spanish summer punch. Peaches are a common addition to sangria, but using white wine gives their flavor more prominence. Don't make this drink terribly sweet; add just enough honey to highlight the peaches. Any leftover punch will still taste great the next night. Replace the sliced peaches with fresh, as they will be too macerated.

yields: 8 (4-ounce) drinks

1   (750-ml) bottle white wine, room temperature
4   ounces (½ cup) brandy, room temperature
2   tablespoons honey
2   ripe white peaches, peeled and sliced
1   lemon, seeded and sliced into rounds

In a large pitcher, combine the wine, brandy, and honey, stirring until the honey dissolves. Stir in the lemon. Cover and refrigerate overnight to allow the flavors to meld.

An hour before serving, stir in the peaches.* Just before serving, taste and add more sugar or honey if needed. If you find it's too sweet, add a little soda water until the desired balance is reached. Serve chilled in wine glasses or over ice in tall glasses.

*To easily peel a peach, purchase a new soft-skin peeler. Or, do as you would a tomato: Mark an X in the bottom of the fruit with a knife. Drop into boiling water for about 30 seconds, and then plunge into ice water to stop the cooking. Starting at the X, peel the skin away from the peach. Cut wedges of fruit from the pit, working over the pitcher to catch any juice.

acapulco sunrise

The Love Boat always stopped in Acapulco, which seems somewhat telling about the possible effects of this drink. It's a slightly different take on the traditional Tequila Sunrise, which is made with tequila, orange juice, and grenadine. The combination of amaretto's almond scent and the tart pucker of grapefruit juice may seem an unlikely pairing, but the flavors meld together intriguingly well. Isaac would be proud.

yields: 1 drink

1 ounce (2 tablespoons) amaretto
½ cup freshly squeezed grapefruit juice
    (1 small or ½ large grapefruit)
1 ounce (2 tablespoons) premium tequila
    Splash of grenadine

Fill a highball glass with ice cubes. Pour the amaretto, grapefruit juice, and tequila over the ice. Add a splash of grenadine, but don't stir. Serve immediately.

bloody mary

When date night turns into date morning, consider this zingy wake-me-up for brunch on the veranda (or 2-square-foot apartment balcony, as the case may be.) Wherever you are, an ice-cold Bloody Mary, perfectly soft-poached eggs topped with snipped chives, crunchy English muffins, and the morning paper will start your day together right.

yields: 1 drink

2 ounces (¼ cup) vodka
4 ounces (½ cup) tomato juice
½ oz (1 tablespoon) freshly squeezed lemon juice
    (½ small lemon)
2 dashes Worcestershire sauce
3 dashes Tabasco sauce
    Salt and freshly ground black pepper to taste
    Lime wedges for garnish
    Celery stalks for garnish

Fill a shaker halfway with ice and add all the ingredients. Shake well. Fill a tall glass with ice, and strain the drink into the glass. Garnish with a wedge of lime and a crisp celery stalk.

kir royale

Champagne cocktails, like this one tinged with black currant, are the height of elegance. For a truly memorable night, pour the Champagne into tall, slender flutes and pour yourself into a sexy little dress! Don't chill your flutes first, as it can dissipate the bubbly.

yields: 1 drink

1   teaspoon crème de cassis or other black currant liqueur
5   ounces chilled Champagne or other sparkling wine
    Lemon twist for garnish

Pour the crème de cassis into the bottom of an unchilled Champagne flute. Slowly fill the flute with chilled Champagne. Garnish with a lemon twist.

vodka martini

To make classic martinis, you'll need a stainless steel cocktail shaker. Look for one at your favorite bottle shop, and then shake, shake, shake until your vodka is icy cold.

yields: 1 drink

2   ounces premium vodka
    Dash of vermouth
3   Picholine green olives

Chill a martini glass in the freezer for at least 10 minutes. Fill a cocktail shaker with ice and pour in the vermouth. Shake well and strain the vermouth into the glass, swirling to coat the sides of the glass. Pour the vodka over the ice in the shaker, and shake well. Strain the vodka into the glass. Spear the olives on a toothpick and add to the drink.

tangerine margaritas

As with candy-like Clementines, tangerines are part of the Mandarin orange family, those easy-to-peel, exceptionally sweet little fruits. Without the tartness of all the lime in a traditional margarita, this drink provides only fresh, fruity fun for the taste buds. Sip alongside a meal of spicy grilled pork tenderloin for a savory-sweet interplay on the palate.

yields: 1 drink

2 tablespoons salt for dipping

2 tablespoons sugar for dipping

1 ounce (2 tablespoons) premium tequila

1 ounce (2 tablespoons) freshly squeezed tangerine juice

2 tablespoons frozen lemonade concentrate

½ ounce (1 tablespoon) Cointreau or other orange-flavored liqueur

   Soda water

   Tangerine slices for garnish

Chill a margarita glass in the freezer for 10 minutes. Combine the salt and sugar on a saucer. Rub the rim of the chilled glass with a wedge of tangerine and then dip the rim into the salt-sugar mixture to coat. Fill the glass with ice. Fill a cocktail shaker with ice, and add the tequila, tangerine juice, Cointreau, and frozen lemonade. Shake well and strain into the glass. Top with a splash of soda water and garnish with a tangerine slice.

mexican hot chocolate

Say goodbye to Swiss Miss. The pinafore has got to go, and in its place is this steamy drink of cinnamony chocolate spiked with just enough red hot chile peppers to remind you you're on date, not sitting with your grandma. Curl your toes with a little added rum or Grand Marnier. Be sure to use chile powder that contains only ground red chile pods for the purest flavor. Look for it in the Mexican foods section of your supermarket.

yields: 2 drinks

2½ cups whole milk

1 teaspoon chile powder, or more to taste

½ vanilla bean, split lengthwise and scraped

4 ounces high-quality unsweetened or bittersweet chocolate, chopped (about ⅔ cup)

   Honey and/or brown sugar to taste

2 cinnamon sticks for stirring

Combine the milk, chile powder, and vanilla bean in a small saucepan and set over medium heat. Cook until it just starts to simmer, and then reduce the heat to low. Add the chocolate and whisk until dissolved completely.

Remove the vanilla bean pod and pour the chocolate into mugs. Stir in honey or brown sugar to taste and garnish with a cinnamon stick.

café brulot

This traditional after-dinner treat from New Orleans is best made with a strong, dark-roasted coffee. It provides a kick of energy after a slow, languorous meal. If you want the flavor without the caffeine, feel free to substitute decaf. The drink will warm you to your toes, and you'll still sleep like a baby. But only if you want to.

yields: 2 drinks

   Peel of ¼ orange
   Peel of ½ lemon
2 teaspoons sugar
2 whole cloves
1 cinnamon stick
2 ounces (¼ cup) Grand Marnier or cognac
8 ounces hot, freshly brewed coffee

Combine the citrus peels, sugar, cloves, cinnamon stick, and liqueur in a small saucepan and set over low heat. Cook for 2 minutes, stirring until the sugar is dissolved. Using a long-handled match, ignite the mixture, then stir in the coffee until the flames subside. (Turn off the lights for full effect.) Ladle the mixture through a sieve into coffee cups and serve immediately.

mulled cider

When autumn rustles in after summer, and outdoor cookouts give way to campfires and nubby sweaters, make a road trip to your local orchard and pick some crisp fruits for the season. Stock up on freshly pressed cider while you're there, and make this drink anytime you want to warm hearth or home or heart.

yields: 2 drinks

6 allspice berries
1 cinnamon stick
1 cup apple cider
⅓ cup freshly squeezed orange juice
½ lemon, sliced
1 teaspoon honey
¼ cup brandy

Combine the allspice, cinnamon, apple cider, orange juice, lemon slices, and honey in a small saucepan and set over medium-high heat. Bring the mixture to a boil, remove the pan from the heat, and stir in the brandy. Ladle the mixture through a sieve into mugs and serve immediately.

date night menus

feed me!
a meal to eat with your hands

There's no good reason why you can't have two or three appetizers for dinner, so go ahead and make a night of these Asian-inspired starters. There's no law that says you have to eat with a fork, either. So remember: licking your fingers (or somebody else's) is perfectly acceptable behavior behind closed doors.

let's have a quickie!
dinner on the table in 15 minutes (or so)

You may think you're too busy or too tired to cook dinner, but this is a meal that pulls together in a flash, made mostly with ingredients you'll have on hand. So go ahead and resurrect a hell of a day with a heavenly meal.

meat-free but full of love:
a vegetarian supper

You and your sweetie may not agree on the morality of eating a slice of crispy bacon but you're sure to find common ground in a platter of pretty bruschetta topped with basil and tomato, roasted red pepper and feta, and goat cheese and honey. Cleanse your palate before the entrée with a simple green salad. The next course goes from fresh to decadent with lasagne stuffed with spinach and mushrooms and dripping with melted cheese. Finish the meal off on a lighter note with whatever fresh fruits and berries are in season.

hot stuff:
dinner for a hot summer night

Fire up the grill as soon as you get home, then cool down with a Frozen Pomegranate Margarita and nibble on guacamole as you whip up a batch of refreshing gazpacho. After you've grilled the steak, warm some corn tortillas on the grill, slice the meat into strips, and make little tacos with some of the guacamole. If you don't have time to make fresh fruit sorbet for dessert, bottom's up to another margarita.

frozen pomegranate margaritas 162

chips and classic guacamole 18

gazpacho 68

grilled flank steak 107

mango sorbet 152

still tasty after all these years:
an anniversary feast

Making a big anniversary dinner is a bit of a production—but that's the point, isn't it? Wait until you both have the day off and then spend a leisurely afternoon together cooking, talking, tasting, and toasting.

pan-fried gruyère cheese 25

pan-seared rib-eye for two 91

blue cheese mashed potatoes 89

red wine-poached pears 148

the perfect pair:
a menu of wine-friendly foods

Experimenting with wine can bring a fun new challenge to your kitchen adventures. For this meal, I recommend you try a Sauvignon Blanc or a dry Chardonnay with the appetizers. Save a little bit of the tapenade to dab on the salmon and see how you like it with a Pinot Noir. When pairing wine with dessert, the wine should be as sweet or sweeter than the dessert, so I like to have a little glass of ripe, fruity Muscat with the pear galette.

antipasto platter 34

kalamata olive tapenade 34

lake como-style salmon 97

almond-pear galette 142

rescue me!
a mid-winter meal to soothe the soul

Instead of roasting the chicken with potatoes, make a batch of smooth, creamy potato leek soup for a first course, then surround the chicken with carrots, baby beets, or a cubed acorn squash. Change into your pajamas after dinner and curl up in front of a fire with a mug of warm cocoa to finish the evening.

potato leek soup 73

baby spinach salad with bacon and swiss 44

roasted chicken 92

mexican hot chocolate 166

spice it up:
an exotic vacation for your tastebuds

When you're tired of playing it safe, try a menu with bold, exciting flavors. Start off slowly with the surprising richness of the cauliflower soup and then let your tastebuds take off on a rollercoaster ride with the lamb vindaloo. Cool down with a scoop of ice cream slowly melting over the sweet wontons.

roasted cauliflower soup 65

lamb vindaloo 111

pumpkin wontons with brown butter-walnut sauce 157

16 super-quick dishes for busy weeknights

Think you have no time for cooking? There's *always* time for date night.
Try these lightning-fast dishes for a home-cooked taste without much effort.

1. While pasta cooks, sauté peeled, deveined shrimp with minced garlic and unsalted butter. Toss the shrimp and pasta with shredded parsley, cilantro, or basil.

2. Rub medallions of pork tenderloin with curry powder, then sauté in peanut oil. Transfer the pork to a plate and simmer some coconut milk in the pan for a quick curry sauce.

3. Broil salmon steaks and top them each with a dollop of fresh Kalamata Olive Tapenade (page 34) or a good-quality store-bought version.

4. Make gourmet BLTs: Fry thin slices of pancetta and stack them with slices of heirloom tomatoes. Tuck fresh arugula between two slices of rustic bread slathered with mayonnaise.

5. Grill flank or skirt steak and slice into thin strips. Serve over mixed greens and top with crumbled blue cheese. Add toasted pecans if you have them.

6. Corn fritters: Add one cup of corn kernels to your favorite pancake recipe and fry in oil. Serve with Salsa Cruda (page 22).

7. Croque Madame. Fry slices of whole wheat bread in butter, turn and cover with slices of Gruyère; cook until the cheese melts. Top each one with a few warm slices of ham and a fried egg.

8. Toss a can of white beans with halved cherry tomatoes, sliced shallots, shredded oregano, sage and/or rosemary, and a simple dressing of olive oil and vinegar.

9. Make burritos with shredded rotisserie chicken breasts, shredded romaine lettuce, and a big dollop of guacamole.

10. Set out an Antipasto Platter (page 34) along with hot fresh rolls and *aïoli* (made from mayonnaise mixed with minced fresh garlic).

11. Cut the stem off an artichoke. Microwave with a bit of water in a covered plastic container for 8 minutes, or until the leaves pull out easily. Serve with the Master Vinaigrette (page 38).

12. Slice a green apple and top each slice with a thin piece of Manchego cheese. Spread a bit of quince paste or fig jam on the cheese. Sprinkle with slivered almonds or serve whole Marcona almonds on the side.

13. Top freshly shucked oysters with minced grapefruit sections and shaved fennel.

14. Combine some Israeli couscous with a can of rinsed white beans, high-quality oil-packed tuna, and chopped parsley, tomato, garlic, and green onions. Spritz with a lemon.

15. Slice some fresh figs in half, top with a small spoon of goat cheese, and wrap with prosciutto. Drizzle with a bit of honey and chopped walnuts.

16. Buy plain store-bought cupcakes and make a homemade quatro-leches sauce of ½ cup each of sweetened condensed milk, evaporated, whipping cream, and light coconut milk. Add some rum, too, if you like. Saturate the cupcakes completely before consuming.

index